GO FOR IT!

●

A Book on Sport and Recreation
for Persons with Disabilities

GO FOR IT!

●

A Book on Sport and Recreation
for Persons with Disabilities

Editors

Jerry D. Kelley, Ph.D
International Alliance on Disability
Washington, D.C.

Lex Frieden
The Institute for Rehabilitation and Research
Foundation and Baylor College of Medicine
Houston, Texas

HBJ

HARCOURT BRACE JOVANOVICH PUBLISHER
Orlando · San Diego · Chicago · Dallas

Go for It! was inspired by the Swedish book *KOM IGEN*, Engström, G. and Augustsson, L. (eds.) (Malmö, Sweden. Liber Förlag, 1985). It was developed as a cooperative project of Bröllopsfondens Publikationsstiftelse and the International Alliance on Disability. Sponsorship was provided by Harcourt Brace Jovanovich, Publishers, the International Alliance on Disability and the Royal Wedding Trust. Additional support was given by the Stuart-James Foundation, James T. Lewis Enterprises, Henry M. Moore and the Institute for Rehabilitation and Research Foundation.

Principal Writers: Elizabeth Defay and Jerry D. Kelley

Photographic Coordination and Selection: Jerry D. Kelley

Design: Production staff of Harcourt Brace Jovanovich, Publishers

CONTENTS

King Carl XVI Gustaf and Queen Silvia
Kingdom of Sweden

I am sure that you who are just starting to read the book *Go for It!* have often felt the intense thrill and excitement of watching a sports event, be it a team sport or one in which athletes are competing as individuals. I am also sure that you have felt a certain admiration for the way in which athletes control their bodies and use their techniques to the utmost.

Sports, however, are more than just brilliant results reached in a competition. Sports involve more than just watching. Taking part in sports activities means stimulation, friendship and growing self-confidence.

The most important thing in competition is not to win but to take part. And it is certainly not only the results in inches and seconds or the score of the game that counts. It is your will to compete, your total engagement, that provides the meaning. Everybody has the same starting point—all you have to do is join in and try.

Participation in sports gives you a chance to experience communion as well as communication. It might be the togetherness with fellow team members or the togetherness among friends in a joyful, fun competition. And when the goal is competition as such and not the results, then sports create ties that know no boundaries.

It was in sports that the word *handicap* was first used. The idea behind the word was to give everybody in a group of contestants the very same chance. Artificial boundaries that keep some from the togetherness of sports should never be allowed. I feel strongly that whatever limits we may have in a physical or mental sense, we can always find a way to take part together.

To take part in sports—through competitions or just training on our own—helps greatly in building self-confidence. All of us have much greater resources than we know or believe, both physically and mentally. But these inner resources have to be activated. Too many of us are afraid to fail—and therefore never try. In these situations, support and encouragement help enormously. When the difficulties seem insurmountable, then we need a friendly push to get over the first hurdle. After that first step, everything is often much easier. Our self-confidence grows, our hesitation diminishes. We feel happiness in having conquered that resistance, that creeping fear within ourselves. We know that our wings will carry us.

The basic content of this book will be presented in many countries at the same time. This demonstrates the importance of the internationalization of sports for the disabled, shown also in the games for disabled athletes in connection with the past Olympic Games in Calgary and Seoul and the Olympic Games which will take place in Barcelona in 1992. International games give athletes with disabilities a chance not only to share the joy of competition with people from other countries but also to exchange experiences as sportsmen and persons with disabilities.

It is my sincere hope that everybody who takes part in sports activities will feel the togetherness, the thrilling stimulation and the constantly growing self-confidence and self-respect that sports provide. I know that this is important for those who have some physical or mental limitations, and that *Go for It!* will serve as an encouragement and signal to go forward.

Silvia

Queen of Sweden
Chairman, Royal Wedding Trust

The President and Mrs. Bush
United States of America

Go for It! is a statement of challenge and encouragement often used in the sports world, and it aptly expresses the spirit and intent of this book.

Over the past decades, people with all types and degrees of physical and mental impairment have moved into the mainstream of sport and recreation, whether in the community recreation center or on the playing fields of national and international competitions. Activities that were once thought to be impossible for some disabled people are now commonplace. *Go for It!* reflects these important changes and encourages all to seek out the activities that best meet individual needs and interests. The book gives simple, straightforward instruction on how the activities are performed and how they may be adapted so that everyone can participate. It is a celebration of past accomplishments and a challenge for the future.

The encouragement for this book came from Her Majesty Queen Silvia of Sweden, a dedicated advocate for sports for the disabled. The idea was carried forward by the International Alliance on Disability and many of the sport and recreation leaders in the United States and Sweden who have worked to create new opportunities for people with disabilities. It is my great pleasure to join with Queen Silvia in applauding these efforts, and I urge that we continue our united commitment to offer all people an equal opportunity for a life enriched by participation in meaningful leisure pursuits.

Barbara Bush

Every four years, the best athletes of the world gather together to compete and share friendship and fraternity in the Olympic Games. These athletes represent the best efforts of the youth of the world.

During the opening and closing ceremonies as well as throughout the competitions, one can witness various men and women athletes in wheelchairs or on crutches. They represent but a very small part of all the disabled athletes in the world who dedicate themselves daily to improving their physical and mental abilities in the same manner as so-called "normal" athletes. Participation in the Olympic Games is perhaps the ultimate recognition and reward they can attain for their extraordinary energy and their strength of character, not to mention their profound determination.

It is unfortunately true that people with disabilities are to a large extent ignored by society and are given only very few occasions in which to prove themselves to the best of their abilities. Sport, on the other hand, is an area in which it is possible to demonstrate to mankind that there are no differences between us. It encourages disabled people to confront their limitations. Sport also constitutes an opportunity for many disabled athletes to obtain the recognition that they so richly deserve.

The International Olympic Committee and the entire Olympic Family is particularly grateful to H.M. Queen Silvia and the Swedish Royal Wedding Trust for the efforts they have made in making this dream a reality and for giving the readers of this publication a true insight into the real meaning of sport for persons with disabilities and its importance in today's world.

Juan Antonio Samaranch
President
International Olympic Committee

Preface

Most people approach life and sport in similar ways. The focus is on individual achievement, cooperation and team effort—everyone is expected to make the best use of his or her natural abilities and attributes. Persons with disabilities are no different; they approach their daily lives on the same basis, and it is on this basis that they wish to be judged. All too often, however, disabled persons are treated as though they are less than complete, and lacking in potential, when in fact having a disability merely means having an altered potential.

Public policy states that everyone, including persons with different types and degrees of functional impairments, should have a full opportunity to participate in all aspects of community life. To bring this policy to fruition, we must create a physical environment in our sport and recreation centers, stadiums, parks and playgrounds that is accessible to everyone, including persons with disabilities.

Sport and recreational activities bring together men and women, children and the elderly, and people of all ethnic, religious, socio-economic and cultural backgrounds in a spirit of fun and interaction.

Sometimes it is for non-competitive play and fellowship—at other times we are spectators or athletes in intensely fought championship competitions. In any case, the sport and recreational setting provides a stimulating atmosphere that contributes to and reflects community integration and solidarity.

The effort to achieve full integration of persons with disabilities is the goal and should be seen in light of each citizen's wish to belong and play a significant role in society. Since sport and recreation is an important part of the community, society prospers when disabled and able-bodied citizens participate together. The physical, psychological and social benefits can be shared equally by all.

A Natural Demarcation

Ever since people began competing in different sport and recreational activities, they have divided themselves into groups or classes according to age, sex or other physical characteristics so as to equalize the competition. For example, weight classes are used in wrestling and weightlifting. In shooting, classification is based on whether shooting is performed in a standing, kneeling or prone position. Thus classification may be based on how the activity is performed or the physical characteristics of the participants.

The personal characteristics warranting classification in all sport and recreation usually warrant classification for persons with disabilities. When accommodations are needed to take into account a disabled participant's special situation or needs, it may be necessary to amend the rules, modify the playing area or surface, or alter distances. For example, sitting volleyball uses a lower net. Because wheelchairs are used in wheelchair basketball, the rules are modified to take into account the presence of wheelchairs, but the court size and length of play remains unchanged.

The person with a disability may be disadvantaged in other ways that need to be considered. Take, for example, the swimmer with an amputated leg. The sport of swimming has not been modified, but a separate classification ensures equality of competition. Another factor to be considered is the use of adapted equipment or aids. For example, a double-amputee skier may use a mono-ski or sit-ski in order to participate. In this case the adaptive equipment affects the classification.

Many persons with disabilities participate without any direct modifications. When modifications are necessary, they should be as minimal as possible so that the activity approximates a *normal* experience.

When an individual participates (alone or in a group) primarily for recreation or exercise, modifications can be adjusted according to the situation and changed as needed. The changes are of little consequence. In competitions, however, certain rules or standards are followed so that (1) all competitors have an equal chance and (2) the activity can be repeated using the same standards. This also becomes important if the individual wants to measure his or her performance against others. To accomplish this purpose, different categories may be established—based on the nature of the disability, the adaptive equipment used and the functional level of the participants.

Currently medical diagnostic categories are used to determine class divisions in many sports, an approach that has created numerous subclasses or divisions. However, some people think that medical diagnosis is not the best way to classify disabled athletes, and that reducing the number of disability classes would make competitive sporting events more interesting and exciting. As a result, several functional classification systems have been developed based on the ability to perform rather than according to medical characteristics.

In spite of special arrangements, some sport and recreational activities always will be less suitable or even impossible for some individuals with disabilities. Not every sport can be adapted. Everyone recognizes this fact.

On the other hand, the history of the sports movement for disabled persons is filled with examples of errors made by well-meaning experts who predetermined that an activity could not be modified, or that it would be impossible for a person with a given disability to participate. Time and again, experts have been proved wrong by the determination or innovative solutions developed by persistent would-be participants.

The individual should always have the opportunity to choose whether or not to participate so that his or her particular wishes are met on the same terms as everyone else.

Sport: An Important Part of Life

Many sporting activities bring together people who share similar experiences and emotions. Even when participants and spectators share a desire for victory over the opposition, they share the same enjoyment of the sport. Futhermore, many sport and recreational activities are based on teamwork and cooperation. The resulting team spirit and mutual respect can positively influence the individual's social, psychological and interpersonal development. This comradeship may be particularly important when a person is struggling to regain self-confidence and self-esteem after a serious injury.

The element of competition in sport and recreation is also valuable. When competing against ourselves, we try to improve our performance to achieve a certain goal. When competing with others, we compare our own performance with that of our competitors and are spurred on by the wish to achieve results that are as good in our next effort, if not better. The perseverance, concentration and self-discipline needed to achieve these objectives are used in every aspect of life.

Benefits also accrue from the aesthetically pleasing and stimulating physical environment of most sport and recreational activities. Outdoor activities such as orienteering, skiing, hiking and canoeing provide an opportunity to combine the wonders of nature and beautiful scenery with the challenge of personal accomplishment.

For persons with disabilities, sport and recreational activities are of special value. They provide an enjoyable and personally rewarding route to improved functioning. Also, participation in sport and recreation plays an important role in the overall rehabilitation process. When carried out under the supervision and watchful eye of a skilled professional, the physical, psychological and social benefits of sport and recreational activities can be structured into individually planned programs that result in predictable therapeutic outcomes. Such programs can be very important to the individual and will probably reduce the time it takes for the person to reach his or her own optimal level of independent functioning.

Go for It! is not about rehabilitation or therapy, however. It is about fun, challenge and the exhilaration that comes with active participation. It introduces the reader to many opportunities available for persons with disabilities. But keep in mind, however, that the possibilities are endless. Go for It!

Sven-Olof Brattgård
Professor of Handicapped Research
Gothenburg University

Hans Lindström
Swedish Handicapped
Sports Federation

Introduction

Go for It! reflects our national commitment to sport and recreation. It describes many opportunities available to persons with disabilities, from highly competitive athletic endeavors to casual games in neighborhood playgrounds, recreation centers and sports clubs. Sport and recreation is for all—able-bodied and disabled—and society has a duty and responsibility to make it possible for everyone to participate.

This book grew out of the commitment of Queen Silvia of Sweden that all persons with disabilities be given an equal chance to enjoy the benefits of sport. *Go for It!* was inspired by the Swedish book, *KOM IGEN*. The original Swedish book was a project of the Royal Wedding Trust—a non-profit foundation created by the King and Queen at the time of their wedding to advance opportunities for disabled persons. Because of *KOM IGEN*'s success, Queen Silvia, who is Chairman of the Royal Wedding Trust, thought that readers in other countries might benefit from adapted versions in their own languages. Currently, editions are available in German and Spanish. The international Alliance on Disability was given the opportunity to prepare this English edition.

While the Swedish Royal Wedding Trust has generously provided us with written materials as well as pictures for use in *Go for It!*, this book should not be viewed as a translation. Unlike the original Swedish version, *Go for It!* is directed primarily to persons with physical and sensory disabilities and includes many activities unique to the American experience. It is similar in purpose in that it describes sport and recreational opportunities available to everyone. It provides information on becoming an active participant, bouncing back after illness or injury and—most of all—discovering that participation is fun and rewarding.

Go for It! is based on the premise that involvement in sport and recreational activities is essential to the health, fitness and psychological well-being of all people, that persons with disabilities should be given the same opportunities to participate as anybody else, and that we all have a responsibility to make these opportunities available.

Many newly disabled persons, their families and friends, and some service providers are not aware of the possibilities that currently exist. Some disabled individuals incorrectly think that possibilities for participation are limited or not available. They may not know how to become involved, or they may not recognize the potential benefits. It is our hope that this book will become a valuable resource to those individuals. Through pictures and print, the book encourages persons with disabilities to become active participants. It is designed to inform, motivate and stress possibilities, not limitations. It describes what sport and recreation offer and how one might go about selecting an activity that fits individual needs and interests.

Many of the content contributors and resource persons are themselves disabled and active sport and recreation participants—indeed, some are distinguished champions. This book is a compilation of their ideas and suggestions. Common to all is the recognition of the importance that sport and recreation has played in their lives, reflecting the encouragement and friendships that have emerged from these experiences.

People who are currently spectators are encouraged to try a sport or recreational activity. *Go for It!* is designed to show them how. It is designed to educate and inform interested parents, family members and service providers—teachers,

recreation leaders and physical educators—about how to assist and support disabled persons through specific information and by example. It also can serve as a valuable supplementary resource for special education teachers, recreation therapists, adapted physical educators and entry-level professionals in hospitals, institutions and rehabilitation facilities. Though the book does not examine activities in terms of treatment or therapy, it is generally accepted that everyone gains certain therapeutic benefits from involvement and participation in sport and recreation.

Go for It!, however, is not just for those who have a direct association with disabilities or for professionals providing services. It is hoped that the book will be of interest and value to the general public. It is estimated that 36 million Americans have some form of disability. If one includes all who will acquire a disability associated with aging, some 50 million Americans will experience an activity-limiting impairment during their lifetimes. An accident or other unexpected event could make any one of us a member of this group at any time. It is almost certain that each of us will know a family member, friend or close acquaintance who has a disability.

Go for It! takes the position that persons with disabilities have the same rights as anybody else. In fact, laws have been passed recently to ensure equal opportunity. While vigilance is required to protect and advance these rights, responsibility for participation ultimately rests with the individual. Each disabled person must seek out the kind of activity that is desired. Also, it is important for the individual to give support to the various organizing groups attempting to advance particular sports.

We are grateful to disabled sport and recreation leaders for their support and assistance in preparing this book. We also are grateful to Queen Silvia and the many disabled sport leaders in Sweden who have so generously assisted us. We hope we have retained the valuable motivational qualities of the original book, and that *Go for It!* will stimulate new experiences in sport and recreation for everyone.

We are also grateful to First Lady Barbara Bush for her readiness to support this effort.

For publishing this book as a service to disabled persons and for committing all profits derived from it for the furtherance of sports opportunities for disabled people, we are especially indebted to Harcourt Brace Jovanovich, Inc.

Finally, we wish to pay tribute to the tens of thousands of disabled athletes who have demonstrated a pioneering spirit and dedicated themselves to opening new doors of opportunity. They have created, adapted and stimulated new ideas, techniques and devices that have enabled themselves and others to move into the mainstream of sport and recreation and, thus, into the mainstream of life.

This spirit is celebrated in *Go for It!*, and it is to this end that the book is dedicated.

Jerry D. Kelley
Lex Frieden
Editors

CHAPTER
1
TEAM SPORTS

Introduction

Team membership provides some of the most important and rewarding learning experiences in life: sharing a common goal with one's teammates; cooperating to achieve team success; making personal sacrifices for the good of all; the joy of victory; yes, even the reinforcement and support needed to deal with defeat. Team sports "enable individuals to savor the thrill of victory and suffer through the agony of defeat, recognizing that there can be defeat in victory and victory in defeat!"[1] This is what family and community life is all about—this is what sport is all about.

Until recent times, persons with disabilities were excluded from these experiences. It wasn't until the late 1940s, when wheelchair basketball burst onto the scene, that people began to recognize the benefits and importance of team sports for disabled athletes. Since that time, virtually all sports have been adapted or modified to accommodate persons with disabilities.

Most accommodations resulted from initiatives by disabled athletes, including disabled war veterans faced with the challenge of building a new life after experiencing paralysis, sensory impairment or loss of limbs. Other accommodations were made by educators, sport leaders and rehabilitation experts who saw sport as a way of encouraging physical recovery and psychological fulfillment.

The goals have always been the same: keep the sport as much like the original as possible; never compromise challenges and risk factors that are basic to the sport; make concessions to limitations resulting from disability only when absolutely necessary; provide classification systems that ensure equitable participation for all. Always encourage side-by-side participation by able-bodied and disabled athletes.

Results have astonished even the most jaded observer. Basketball,

football, soccer, softball, volleyball, goalball, beep baseball—the list goes on and on. All are extremely popular team sports enjoyed by participants and spectators alike. The sports presented in this book only begin to suggest the possibilities.

As Thomas Carlyle wrote, "Let each become all that he was created capable of being. Expand, if possible, to his full growth, and show himself at length in his own shape and stature." Team membership and dedication to excellence in sport enable a person to become what he or she was created to be. Such experiences apply to the quest for a fuller life.

If a team sport that strikes your personal fancy is not described in the following chapter, don't be discouraged. At local, national and international levels, groups and organizations are dedicated to the development or advancement of virtually every sport. Of course, some sports are more popular and have advanced more quickly than others, but you will surely be able to find one that fits your interests.

Beep Baseball[2]

Baseball is a consuming American passion. Just mentioning Babe Ruth, Joe DiMaggio, Mickey Mantle, Willie Mays or Hank Aaron will spark a heated debate about who was the greatest player of all time. Even people who don't care about sports often know how many home runs Babe Ruth hit in a single season and who won the last World Series.

During evening hours and on weekends, millions of Americans charge out onto the playing fields or sandlots when they hear the umpire's cry of "Play ball!" Whether old or young, rich or poor, black or white, male or female, most Americans love baseball.

Until very recent times, the joys of playing baseball could not be experienced by visually impaired and blind athletes. But in 1964, an engineer named Charley Fairbanks placed a small electronic module in a ball, creating a baseball that beeped. His fellow engineers, who formed a group known as the Telephone Pioneers of America, devised a set of cone-shaped, knee-high rubber bases that contain electrically powered sounding units that emit high-pitched whistles. After a few adaptations to the rules of regular baseball, the game of beep baseball was born.

The popularity of the game was slow to develop because of unreliable equipment, but by the mid-1970s, technical problems were solved, new rules were devised by blind athletes to make the game more competitive and the first World Series game was held in St. Paul, Minnesota, before a cheering throng of spectators.

Understanding the game is relatively easy. A game lasts six innings unless more are needed to break a tie. Like regular baseball, a team has three outs per inning. Unlike regular baseball, there is no second base, and batters are given five strikes while hitting instead of three. First and third bases are placed 90 feet down their respective lines, and 5 feet outside the foul line to prevent runners from colliding with defensive players. Bases contain electrical units that give off a buzzing sound when activated. The batter does not know which one will be activated when he or she steps into the batter's box. When the ball is hit, the umpire activates one of the bases. The batter must identify and run to the correct base before the defensive players field the ball. If the runner reaches the base before the ball is fielded, a point is scored. There is no running between bases.

Each team is made up of six visually impaired fielders, a sighted pitcher and a sighted catcher. Fielders with some sight must wear a blindfold. The pitcher attempts to place

James Mastro

James Mastro has been involved in sports all his life, even though he was blinded in an accident when he was a teenager. His record of achievement in sports is impressive: In 1976, he was an alternate member of the United States Olympic Wrestling Team, and over the last decade he has won numerous shot-put, discus and goalball medals in the Pan American Games for the Blind and the International Games for the Disabled. He also finished among the top three in 1974, 1975 and 1976 in national Greco-Roman wrestling competitions (able-bodied) sponsored by the Amateur Athletic Union.

Mastro is also a judo enthusiast and an avid beep baseball and goalball player—he has played for seven years on the All-Tournament Team of the National Beep Baseball Association, and was named most valuable player in 1978, 1979 and 1980. Mastro also coaches high school wrestling at Edison High School in Minneapolis, works for the Braille Sports Foundation and teaches adapted physical education at the University of Minnesota. Mastro was the first blind person in the United States to earn a doctoral degree in physical education.

Mastro has strong feelings about the importance of sports for people with disabilities: "Sports are extremely important in society today—consider media coverage of baseball, football, Wide World of Sports, golf, tennis and the Olympics. If disabled people are not involved, they miss out on a large aspect of society. Disabled individuals have a right to as normal a life as possible, and sports participation is part of normal life."

the ball so that it can be hit by the batter. Before pitching the ball, the pitcher shouts *ready*, and when the ball is released, shouts *pitch*. The sighted pitcher and catcher do not get a turn at bat. When their team is on defense, they position themselves in the outfield behind the fielders and give oral directions to help the fielders locate the batted ball. They are not permitted to field the ball themselves.

Today, hundreds of visually disabled athletes enjoy a sport that was once the exclusive domain of sighted players. It is a team sport that is fun to play and offers a variety of challenges. One of beep baseball's greatest contributions, however, is the bridge it creates between sighted and visually disabled athletes. During recreational games, sighted people often put on a blindfold and join in. They go away from a beep baseball game with a better appreciation of what blindness is all about, having participated with or witnessed athletes overcoming a visual disability. Visually disabled athletes go home with the joy and satisfaction that comes from playing the game known as "the great American pastime."

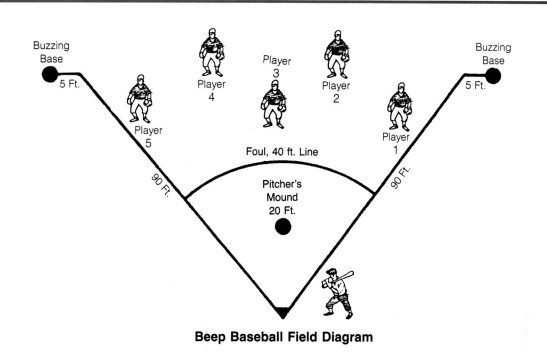

Beep Baseball Field Diagram

Wheelchair Basketball

Basketball is a popular and fiercely competitive sport in the United States and many other parts of the world. Virtually every high school and college in the United States has a team, and many games are broadcast on national or local television. National Basketball Association (NBA) professional games attract large crowds and considerable attention from the media. Indeed, basketball is one of the most popular sports for participants and spectators alike.

Wheelchair basketball is the most popular team sport played by disabled athletes in the United States. It is the only wheelchair team sport played worldwide and ranks as the oldest organized wheelchair sport in the world—the National Wheelchair Basketball Association (NWBA) was created in 1949. The first international wheelchair basketball competition was held in England in 1956 at the International Stoke Mandeville Games.

Athletes play wheelchair basketball because it is fun, good exercise and competitive. Every team in the country fits on a continuum somewhere between the for-fun-only team and the most elite competitive sport team. It is also a popular spectator sport— large national and international multi-sport competitions often end with wheelchair basketball games as their grand finale. The excitement of the game usually keeps the spectators from leaving until the very end of the competition.

"We don't want the public to view us as brave or courageous. We want to be recognized for our skill. That's what I keep working for."

David Kiley
(Paraplegic)
Wheelchair Athlete

Basic basketball rules apply to wheelchair basketball. The biggest difference is that the chair is considered part of the player, and contact with the chair is considered a foul. No special facilities are required, just a basketball court or any hard surface where there is a backboard and hoop.

Competition and Player Eligibility

Anyone who has a permanent, severe leg disability and who can hold a basketball while handling a wheelchair can play in NWBA-sanctioned competitions. Persons with severe hearing impairments can play regular basketball, either on able-bodied teams or with a league sponsored by the American Athletic Association for the Deaf. Persons with single-leg amputations play regular basketball using a prosthetic leg or play wheelchair basketball; double amputees play wheelchair basketball. A number of disability organizations sponsor wheelchair basketball competitions, as do colleges and universities.

Classification System Used by the National Wheelchair Basketball Association (NWBA)

Class I: Complete spinal paraplegia at T-7, or above, or comparable disability that severely limits trunk mobility and balance and arm strength and range of motion. (1 value point)

Class II: Complete motor loss at T-8 to L-2 or comparable disability (including double hip amputees) that limits forward, backward and sideward trunk mobility and balance. (2 value points)

Class III: All other ambulatory disabilities, including lower limb amputations. (3 value points)

The NWBA classification system is undergoing intensive—and heated—review, both in the United States and internationally. The current system is derived from a medical description of spinal cord injury. A movement is afoot to develop a functional classification that reflects each player's physical capabilities to play basketball, as judged by certified classifiers, regardless of medical classification.

Level of Spinal Cord Injury

The severity and nature of spinal cord injuries depend on the location of the spinal cord lesion. Cervical lesions cause various degrees of quadriplegia; thoracic, lumbar and sacral lesions cause various degrees of paraplegia.

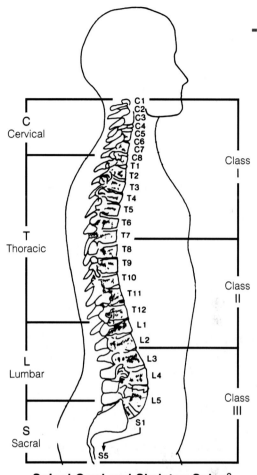

Spinal Cord and Skeleton Spine[3]

Some players use the wheelchair only when involved in wheelchair basketball games. When off the playing floor, they walk unaided or with the help of assistive devices. In fact, in Canada the sport is so popular that it often includes able-bodied athletes who use wheelchairs only during play.

Player classification systems ensure that each team is approximately equal in terms of the severity of the disabilities of the five players on the court. The classification system ensures that severely disabled players participate; this makes it easier to expand interest in the sport and provides a larger pool of players to form new teams. It also helps maintain high standards of competition and strong spectator interest.

Under the NWBA classification system, players on the court must total 12 points or less. Also, no more than three Class III players (those with less impairment) can play on the same team at the same time.

Equipment: The Wheelchair

Players use wheelchairs especially designed for wheelchair basketball. The chair is lightweight, about 14 to 20 pounds—a standard chair weighs about 30 pounds. The chair usually has covered spokes, since the chair takes a lot of abuse during play and spokes are often damaged. Wheels are canted to improve turning ability and make physical contact more difficult. Ball bearings that roll with little friction are used to improve speed.

Rules and Strategy

Rules closely follow National Collegiate Athletic Association (NCAA) rules. Game strategy is essentially the same, except the wheelchair is regarded as part of the player—a personal foul is called if a player charges into an opponent's chair. Game strategies also reflect the fact that wheelchairs can't move sideways. A pick and roll, used to screen a defensive player, is a preferred offensive tactic that enables the player to make a fast break to the basket or gain an open position for a shot.

There are four major differences in rules between stand-up and wheelchair basketball:

- An offensive player is allowed 5 seconds rather than 3 seconds in the lane while the player's team is in possession of the ball.
- In wheelchair basketball, the player can dribble, stop and dribble again. In stand-up basketball, when a player stops dribbling, the ball must be passed or a shot attempted. In wheelchair basketball, a player may take 2 pushes on the wheels. The player must then pass, shoot or coast. He must dribble the ball to the floor before the third push. Three pushes without a dribble is a traveling violation.
- To help equalize physical capabilities, a physical advantage foul is called if a player uses a functional leg or stump to raise off the chair to gain an advantage over an opponent, such as during rebounds or jump balls. Three such fouls disqualify a player from the game. For each foul a free throw is awarded to the offended team and the ball is turned over, out of bounds. Technical and unnecessary roughness fouls are also enforced as in stand-up basketball.
- Defensive players who commit a personal foul in the opponent's backcourt are charged with a backcourt foul. The offended player is awarded two free throws.

Conditioning and Training

Training focuses on strength, flexibility, endurance and developing offensive and defensive concepts and shooting accuracy. Good conditioning also reduces injuries during play. Players practice dribbling while running laps at various speeds, and sprints are sometimes practiced up steep ramps to build endurance. Since wheelchair athletes are prone to hand blisters, they need a lot of practice to toughen their hands during the early part of the season.

Boccia

Boccia is a very popular sport in Europe, particularly in Scandinavia. Boccia's origins are in the French game of *boule*. The game can be played both indoors and outdoors.

Boccia can be played by individuals or with teams of three players, one of whom is the captain. Each team has six leather or wooden balls of one color, usually green or red, which are rolled at a small, white target ball. The object is for each team, taking turns, to get their balls closest to the target ball; points are awarded based on how close each team's balls are to the target ball. The players are lined up at one end of the playing area; only referees are allowed on the court. In an official game, six rounds are played. During each round, each team member rolls two balls.

The playing court measures 12.5 × 6 meters, although in unofficial games, courts of varying size can be used. The playing surface is a flat and smooth floor, such as a tile or wooden gym floor or asphalt surface.

Nearly everyone can play boccia,

especially indoor boccia. International competitions are held for cerebral-palsied participants. The game requires concentration, coordination and balance, as well as teamwork and cooperation.

Curling

Curling is one of the most ancient sports in the world. The Scots played lawn bowling centuries ago, and it is possible curling was invented as a version of bowling on ice. In those days crude, natural boulders were used, drilled with a hole where a player could insert a thumb to give the rock a twist and make it curl across the ice. A curling stone with handles attached, bearing the date 1551, was discovered near Stirling, Scotland, in the early part of this century.

Although today Scotland is the home of the game, in recent decades curling has become an immensely popular sport in Switzerland and Norway. Numerous clubs play regularly in the United States, Canada and France, and World Curling Championships are held each year. Indoor curling is played mainly in Scandinavia and is particularly popular in Sweden.

"I had been too timid to try new things that seemed so unrealistic due to my physical disability. When [we] worked together, it was easy."[4]

Participant Comment
1987 Wilderness Inquiry
Participant

Indoor curling is played individually or as a team on a slightly rough carpet with six large plastic *stones* of two different colors. Each team member, one at a time, throws a stone at a target point within a circle until all six stones are played. The referee decides which team is nearer the target point in the circle. The winning team gets one point for each stone that is closer than the opposing team's stones to the target point. The highest possible score for a single round is 3 to 0; six rounds make a game. The same rules apply for individual play.

Indoor curling can be played either sitting or standing. There are two classes, one for visually disabled players and one for all other players. Visually disabled players use an acoustic signal to direct them to the center point of the target. The game requires muscle strength and endurance, balance, concentration, teamwork and attention to tactics.

The weight of the curling stone makes it difficult for people with reduced arm and hand function to participate. A game called junior curling uses lightweight equipment and can be played by persons with limited upper trunk and limb strength.

Wheelchair Football

Football's popularity in the United States is primarily related to its importance as a collegiate and professional sport that attracts huge audiences and loyal fans, most of whom do not play the game. However, young men throughout the country play competitive football while in high school and college. Gallaudet University fields an all-hearing-impaired team that competes with other colleges in tackle football. In recent years they have been joined by wheelchair players for a different version of the game.

Wheelchair users play touch football at the University of Illinois' Armory Fieldhouse on a Tartan (hard rubber) surface field. The playing field measures 60 × 30 yards with 8-yard end zones. Each team has 6 playing members on the field at a given time, in contrast to the 11-member squads that participate in

tackle football. A two-handed touch substitutes for the tackle; ramming of wheelchairs constitutes blocking. Needless to say, this can be a very rough sport.

Wheelchair football demands routine physical conditioning, teamwork, agility in handling a wheelchair at top speed and the stamina to take hard knocks and trauma. The teams have a number of standard plays, including sweeps, traps, deep passes and screen passes, just as in regular football. Players are instructed in techniques for falling out of their chairs (which occurs often) and in

PROFILE

Max Cleland

Max Cleland has always loved sports. In high school in Lithonia, Georgia, he starred in baseball, basketball, tennis and swimming. His ambition to excel helped in his struggle to survive after a grenade explosion in Vietnam destroyed his right arm and both of his legs.

Following rehabilitation, Cleland decided to enter politics. He served in the Georgia State Senate and in 1977 was appointed by President Carter to serve as the youngest man ever to head the Veterans Administration. Currently, Cleland is Georgia's Secretary of State.

Although Cleland's official duties do not allow him to be active in organized sports, he constantly encourages disabled people to discover the value of participating. For example, he recently used the opportunity presented by Handicapped Awareness Day in Georgia to play wheelchair basketball on a team made up of able-bodied local celebrities who played in wheelchairs against a team of disabled athletes. Cleland scored the most baskets!

Cleland expresses the importance of sports for people with disabilities this way: "For people who are disabled, success in sports doesn't always mean winning. It does always mean trying. Victory is more than scoring points—it's scoring personal triumphs."

procedures for touching ballcarriers as a substitute for full-body tackles.

The limited growth of wheelchair football is directly related to a lack of suitable playing fields. However, the tough young wheelchair athletes who participate would like to see expanded opportunities. No other wheelchair sport affords the same thrill of rough-and-tumble action.

"On the fields of friendly strife are sewn seeds that on other days in other fields will bear the fruits of victory."

Douglas MacArthur
Inscribed on gymnasium at West Point

Goalball

Goalball is a relatively new but highly popular team sport for blind and visually impaired people. A Paralympic sport for men's and women's teams, the game originated in West Germany as a game for blind veterans after World War II. It is widely and enthusiastically played in the United States, where several major cities have teams.

Goalball is a fast-paced sport played on a gymnasium floor by two teams of three players each. The game requires good coordination, concentration, speed, auditory skills, cooperation and teamwork. The object of the game is for each team to roll a ball, made audible by a bell or beeping device, past the opponent's goal line while the opposing team takes defensive measures. A thrown ball may bounce, but it must be rolling before it reaches the opponent's throwing area, or it becomes an infraction. The entire team helps with defense—players can block the ball from a standing, crouching,

kneeling or lying position, using any body part or the whole body. A point is scored each time the ball passes the goal line. Each game lasts 10 minutes, divided by a 3-minute break between halves.

The court consists of a rectangle 18 meters in length and 9 meters wide. It is marked with thick tape or cord so that players can feel their positions. Team members wear a helmet, mouthpiece, elbow pads and blindfold. Visually impaired and sighted participants can play together on an equal basis; however, only visually impaired players participate in championship competitions. No classification system is used, but men and women play separately.

Wheelchair Softball

Softball is a recreational adaptation of baseball, the oldest professional sport in the United States. The primary difference between softball and baseball is that in softball the ball is larger and is pitched underhand to the batter. Wheelchair softball is played with a 16-inch ball on a field modified to smaller proportions of the diamond-shaped field used in baseball.

An adaptation of slow-pitch softball, wheelchair softball has been played in informal competitions at the University of Illinois since the 1950s. The first national tournament was held by the sport's national governing body, the National Wheelchair Softball Association, in 1977.

Wheelchair softball is played according to the American Softball Association's official rules for 16-inch slow-pitch softball, with a few minor modifications. All participants must be in wheelchairs, and the chairs must have foot platforms. The game is played on a smooth, hard surface, such as a large empty parking lot. First base is 30 × 15 inches, half of it placed in foul territory to help prevent collisions between the runner and the defensive player; second and third bases are 15 inches square with a flat surface; a 4-foot-diameter circle is located around each base. A defen-

> *"The aim of the Stoke Mandeville Games is to unite paralyzed men and women from all parts of the world in an international sports movement. And your spirit of true sportsmanship today will give hope and inspiration to thousands of paralyzed people. No greater contribution can be made to society by the paralyzed than to help, through the mechanism of sport, to further friendship and understanding among nations."*
>
> Inscribed on the sport stadium in Aylesbury, England, site of the Stoke Mandeville World Wheelchair Games

sive player must have at least one wheel within the circle to force a runner out. All infielders must keep at least one wheel inside a restraining line until the ball leaves the pitcher's hand. The restraining lines are marked 12 feet behind the bases running parallel to the baselines.

Like wheelchair basketball, wheelchair softball employs a point system to ensure team balance. NWBA Class I, II and III players count for 1, 2 and 3 points respectively. National Wheelchair Athletic Association quadriplegic class (IA, IB, IC) players count 1 point. Players totaling no more than 22 points may be in the lineup at any time. At least one quadriplegic player must be included.

Wheelchair softball is rapidly gaining in popularity around the world. Team size, however, is an inhibiting factor in the growth of the sport.

Seated Volleyball

Volleyball is a sport invented by a YMCA instructor, William G. Morgan, at Springfield College in 1895. Thirty-five years passed before an official rules committee was formed, and it was 69 years before the first Olympic competition was held in 1964. Although volleyball was introduced in Europe during the first part of this century, it did not become popular until Americans fighting in Europe demonstrated the game by avidly playing it in their free time.

While volleyball in the United States is primarily a recreational activity played in back yards or on the beach, the Europeans adopted the game after World War II and turned it into a fiercely competitive sport with practiced finesse and serious strategy. In international competition the U.S. is catching up and is home of the current men's Olympic volleyball champions.

Seated volleyball, an adaptation of the game for disabled people, has been played in Scandinavia for many years; it was first introduced in international championships in 1980. The rules are basically the same as in regular volleyball. The main difference is that the net is lower, about 45 inches high, and the playing court is just 6 × 10 meters. The only significant difference in the rules is that the players sit, and one thigh must always be resting on the floor when the ball is hit. There are no classes or groups, but the game is very difficult for people with poor balance in sitting.

Seated volleyball provides training in coordination, speed, balance, teamwork, fitness and tactics. The skilled player must be able to move quickly across the floor while maintaining good balance. The hands must be kept flat on the floor so that the player can take off quickly and move across to an opening. Players must learn to pass and hit the ball with one or both hands.

Soccer
and Rugby

By all accounts, the most popular spectator sport in the world is soccer. An estimated one billion people around the world watched a recent World Cup match on television.

Soccer apparently originated in England, where the game was once played in meadows and through village streets. Everyone joined in and fought for the ball by both fair means and foul. Three separate sports emerged from this mob pastime. The dribbling game, in which players use their feet or head to get the ball into the goal, became soccer. The carrying game grew into rugby and, in the United States, American football.

Ambulatory Soccer[5]

Ambulatory soccer is sponsored by the American Cerebral Palsy Athletic Association (ACPAA) for athletes with cerebral palsy who are less severely impaired (Classes 6, 7 and 8). Ambulatory soccer is played exactly as regular soccer, except that each team must have at least one Class 6 player and no more than four Class 8 (least severely impaired) players. Although regular soccer rules are followed and no special accommodations are made for ambulatory soccer, coaches consider a number of factors when preparing players for competition.

An important consideration is fitness—players run continuously for 40 minutes during a game. Building up endurance requires rigorous training. Players with cerebral palsy may have been excluded from physical education classes and community-based soccer leagues during their youth, and so may lack fundamental kicking and dribbling skills. Often, training must begin with these fundamentals. Sight (especially visual perception problems), hearing, balance and coordination impairments also should be considered when developing training strategies and determining player positions. Headgear is recommended for players with balance difficulties, who may find themselves frequently on the ground ducking opponents' feet.

Wheelchair Soccer[6]

Wheelchair soccer has been played with enthusiasm by wheelchair athletes with cerebral palsy since 1979. The game is played similarly to foot soccer, except that all players are in manual wheelchairs and the ball is passed, caught, dribbled and thrown with the hands rather than kicked with the feet.

Wheelchair soccer is played on a basketball or similar playing court with a 13-inch playground ball. Each team consists of nine players, usually two goalies, two defensive players, and five offensive linemen. As in other sports, fundamentals are the key to successful wheelchair soccer: passing, catching, dribbling and wheelchair handling. For many players, wheelchair soccer is their first exposure to team sports and the development of offensive and defensive strategies. As such, soccer is invaluable training in the pleasures and hardships of team play.

In many communities, too few players are available to offer opportu-

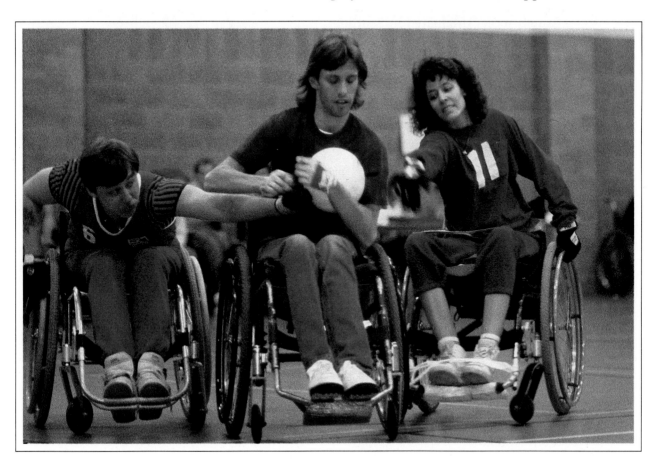

nities for competitive games. To overcome this shortage of players, some wheelchair teams have invited competitions with able-bodied teams. Wheelchairs are provided and rules are modified somewhat to equalize competition. With a little imagination, everyone can play!

"The less fit an individual is, the more stressful it's going to be to operate a wheelchair."

Roger M. Glaser
Physiologist
Wright State University

Crutch Soccer

Crutch soccer originated in Seattle, Washington, in the early 1980s with a group of disabled skiers trying to stay in shape during the off-season. Don Bennett, one of the members of the group, suggested that instead of just doing calisthenics and jogging, kicking a soccer ball around might be fun. The idea caught on, and soon the additional benefits derived from this "new-found activity" led the participants to an enthusiastic commitment to the game of soccer.

Soon, crutch soccer was catching on all over the world. There are numerous programs underway in the United States, Canada, Latin America, Great Britain and the Soviet Union, with Norway, Germany and other nations in the process of developing teams. In addition to acquiring the benefits of fun and physical fitness, each team strives to represent their city (or country) in the World Cup Tournament held annually.

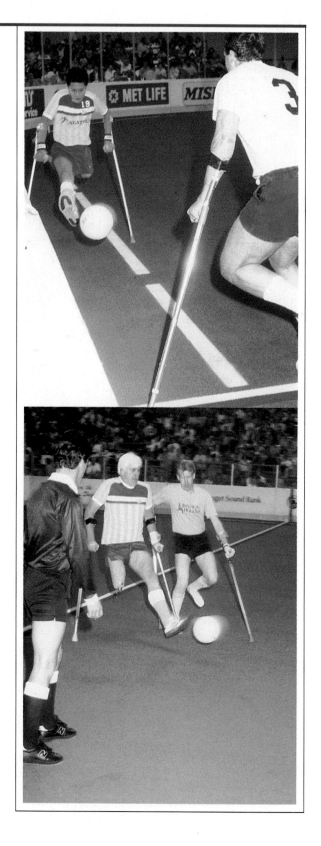

Player Eligibility and Adaptive Equipment

Anyone can play crutch soccer, but most players are amputees. Standard Canadian forearm crutches are used by all field players (able-bodied and disabled), but they may not be used for any purpose other than providing mobility support to the player. Able-bodied players must conform to the same rules as the disabled players.

A kicking leg is selected by each field player, which is not difficult for a person missing a leg. The other leg, or any part of it, is off limits. Using it to intentionally strike or trap the ball is penalized by giving the opposing team a free kick. The rule is intended to prevent a person with a complete or partial second leg from having an advantage over a player with a short or nonexistent residual limb. Able-bodied players must declare their kicking leg at the beginning of the game and then hold their nonplaying foot off the ground, keeping it uninvolved while the ball is in play.

"I think the sports circuit itself is great because it helps build self-esteem, because you're developing your physical powers and your coordination and mobility. . . . I've never seen such a smorgasbord of healthy people in my life as I have at the National Wheelchair Games."[7]

Mary Wilson
(Spinal Cord Injury)

The goalkeeper is usually a person with a single or bilateral upper-limb amputation or some other upper-extremity disability. Just as the field players must declare a kicking leg, the goalkeeper must declare a defending arm (if any), and the other arm (all or part) becomes off-limits. If the nonplaying arm is intentionally used to defend against a goal shot, the opposing team gets a penalty kick. To neutralize a potential leg advantage, the goalkeeper may not, under any circumstances, leave the large penalty zone around the goal to play the ball. But within their prescribed zone, goalkeepers are allowed to use any part of their bodies (except a designated nonplaying limb) to defend the goal and may not be challenged once they have obtained control of the ball. The one-armed goalkeeper gains control of the ball by holding it to the ground with one hand (the foot may not be used). Goalkeepers who do not have the use of either hand gain control of the ball by holding it to the ground with one foot.

Rules and Strategy Basic soccer rules have been modified slightly to accommodate crutches. First, crutches are considered an extension of the arm and may not be used to bat the ball or obstruct another player. If a player intentionally hits the ball with a crutch, the other team is awarded a free kick. Slide tackles are prohibited for obvious safety reasons.

Throwing the ball into play from the sidelines is a bit difficult while standing on one leg with crutches hanging from the arms. Therefore, the ball is kicked in from the sidelines when it goes out of bounds.

Because of the strong physical demands of the sport, unlimited substitutions are allowed to prevent overexertion. Of course, this also provides an opportunity for all players on the team to see action.

Crutch soccer is a co-ed sport involving male and female players ranging in age from 8 to 60 years. For more information on the official rules, how to start a program in your area, or dates for the World Cup tournament, contact Amputee Soccer International.

Quad Rugby[8]

Quad rugby, the only sport exclusively for persons with quadriplegia, is a rapidly developing sport in the United States. Its roots are in wheelchair basketball and ice hockey; its aggressive nature is suggested by its original name, murderball.

Quad rugby was developed by three Canadians from Winnipeg, Manitoba, as the quadriplegic equivalent of wheelchair basketball. It was introduced to the United States in 1981 by Brad Mikkelson, who organized the first team, the Wallbangers, with the assistance of the University of North Dakota's Disabled Student Services. Mikkelson also changed the game's name from murderball to quad rugby.

The game is played with a volleyball on a basketball court with two restricted zones (about 5 feet deep by 24 feet long) delineated on each end. Two teams of four players each attempt to score points by carrying the volleyball across the opposing team's end line.

Player Classification The rules enable quadriplegic players of all abilities to participate on an equal level in quad rugby. A maximum of 12 players are allowed per team; four players are permitted on the court during play. Substitutions are made as in basketball.

As with wheelchair basketball, a team balance rule allows different levels of quadriplegic players to participate fully. The classification system used by the National Wheelchair Athletic Association applies, with some adjustments for trunk stability. Team member classifications on the court must total not more than 8 points: The most impaired players are assigned 1 point, the least impaired, 3 points.

Rules and Strategy Up to three offensive players are allowed in the restricted zone for 10 seconds each; a fourth offensive player in the zone is a violation. The ball handler is allowed unlimited pushes, but must bounce or pass the ball within 10 seconds. Offensive penalties usually result in loss of possession of the ball. Time in a penalty box is the result of most defensive penalties and some other violations.

Defensive strategy usually involves either full-court defense, in which the objective is to press the offense into an error, or defense of the restricted zone. Zone defense focuses on physically taking the ball, forcing the offense to turn the ball over by boxing an offensive player in the zone for more than 10 seconds or by pressuring a bad pass.

Because of the rapid growth of this exciting new sport, adherents expect international competition at the Stoke Mandeville Games in 1990. A starter package for new teams is offered by the United States Quad Rugby Association. It includes a videotape of a game in play, official rules and training and strategy tips. For more information contact the United States Quad Rugby Association.

Portions of this chapter were derived from materials provided by Bill Barry, Ray Clark, Tommy Jacobsson and Stan Labanowich.

REFERENCES

[1] Stein, J. (ed.). *Values of Physical Education, Recreation, and Sports for All* (Reston, VA: American Alliance for Health, Physical Education, Recreation and Dance, Unit on Programs for the Handicapped), p. 15.

[2] National Beep Baseball Association. Adapted from *The NBBA Guide* (NBBA, 9623 Spencer Highway, La Porte, Texas 77571, September 1981).

[3] Sherrill, C. *Adapted Physical Education and Recreation—A Multidisciplinary Approach*, 3rd ed. (Dubuque, IA: Wm. C. Brown Publishers, 1987), p. 161.

[4] Wilderness Inquiry II Annual Report, p. 4.

[5] Roberts, P. Derived from "Ambulatory Soccer." In Jones, J. A. (ed.), *Training Guide to Cerebral Palsy Sports*, 2nd ed. (New York: National Association of Sports for Cerebral Palsy, 1984), pp. 74–76.

[6] Jones, J. and Mushett, M. P. Derived from "Wheelchair Soccer." In Jones, J. A. (ed.), *Training Guide to Cerebral Palsy Sports*, 2nd ed. (New York: National Association of Sports for Cerebral Palsy, 1984), pp. 77–81.

[7] Corbett, B. *Options: Spinal Cord Injury and the Future* (Denver: A. B. Hirschfeld Press, 1980), p. 68.

[8] Dimsdale, A. and Beck, A. Derived from "Reserved for Quads," *Sports 'n Spokes*, 14:2 (1988), pp. 28–30.

CHAPTER
2
INDIVIDUAL SPORTS

Introduction

Whether climbing a mountain, running a race, shooting the rapids, scoring a touchdown or learning a new dance step, most people around the world are captured by the thrill and challenge of participating in some form of sport or recreational activity. For some it may mean striving for competitive excellence— "going for the gold"; for others, it may mean reaching for a personal best, never caring how individual performance is measured against a competitor. Still others may be motivated by a desire to get some exercise and perhaps become more active in the social life of their communities.

Regardless of motivation, every person—including those with disabilities—has a right to pursue his or her own dreams and desires through activities that enrich daily living. This chapter on individual sports presents some possibilities. In many of these sports, participants initiate their own actions independently, set their own goals and are accountable only to themselves for the level of success

achieved. On the other hand, when individuals play with a partner in doubles matches in tennis, racquetball or table tennis, the sport takes on some of the characteristics of a team effort.

It can be said that immediate, objective feedback about success and the opportunity for individual accountability determine much of the appeal of many of these sports. Golfers, bowlers, archers and marksmen try to better previous individual scores whether they win or lose a contest. Results are clear and direct— players know immediately whether and how well they hit the green, the pins or the bull's-eye. They don't have to rely on teammates to decide when they play, what the team goals are or what the strategies should be. In most cases, all they need is one other player who is willing to be the opponent. In some cases the sport can be played alone.

Many of these sports also offer lifelong opportunities for recreation and competition. Whereas few people play team sports such as basketball, soccer or football into their seventies, many people shoot, bowl, golf, play tennis or practice archery throughout their lifetime. This is a particularly valuable and appealing characteristic of the sports described in this chapter.

The socially interactive playing environment associated with individual sports also appeals to many people. Marilyn Hamilton, a champion skier, took up wheelchair tennis because she wanted to be "with the movers and shakers." The tennis court is where she found them. Practice and training almost always take place in a setting that lends itself to building friendships.

Local, state, national and international competitions also afford opportunities for travel and making new acquaintances. Ask any sport enthusiast—social interaction and comradeship add to the pleasure and challenge of the activity.

Success in individual sports requires concentration, skill (especially eye-hand coordination) and practice. Most individual sports improve fitness, coordination, balance and stamina. There are other important benefits, however. Björn Hedman, a physician and chairman of the Medical Committee of the Swedish Handicapped Sports Federation, has written that the athlete, by mobilizing latent physical and mental resources, adds to a fundamental feeling of well-being that comes with increasing knowledge and control of the body. He adds that sports provide a "unique opportunity to bring harmony between body and mind."[1]

The following sections describe how, with just a little ingenuity and considerable determination and practice, disabled people can participate and achieve competence in their sport of choice.

"Disabled people need worthwhile leisure time activities as much or even more than nondisabled people. Leisure activities give some zest to living and provide a common ground for disabled and nondisabled people to meet and become acquainted while concentrating on an activity instead of their differences."[2]

Anne H. Carlsen
Administrator
Crippled Children's School
Jamestown, N.D.

Archery

According to historians, the bow and arrow have been used for over 70 centuries for warfare and hunting. Today archery is classified solely as a sport. Target practice is the most frequent form, although bow-and-arrow hunting is a well-developed sport in many parts of the country.

The most common archery activity is target shooting on a fixed course. In informal matches, any number of arrows at any distance may be shot. In competitive archery, events called rounds involve a fixed number of arrows at specified distances. Since the bow and arrow is a dangerous weapon, safety should always be a prime concern of archers.

Archery is an excellent sport because it is suitable for people of all ages and for those with disabilities. In addition, it is one of the sports in which disabled competitors compete on an equal basis with able-bodied competitors.

For example: An amputee archer with one arm off at the shoulder shoots by using his teeth to fire the arrow; an individual who does not have the use of his arms draws and releases the bow with his feet; an elderly man with limited trunk and abdominal strength and control turns the bow sideways so that he shoots as though using a crossbow; a visually disabled competitor uses an electronic sensing device to hone in on the bull's-eye.

A number of disabled archers are champion competitors in regular archery events. In Sweden, for example, national archery records are held by disabled archers. Bodil Elgh, a wheelchair user, dominates ladies' archery. Patrik Norstrom, born with-

out arms, is one of the three best archers in Sweden today. He wears a specially designed jacket and uses a cleverly constructed system of cords that enables him to use his foot to fire the arrow after he has aimed. Susan Hagel, a wheelchair athlete from Minnesota, has won several indoor and outdoor state tournaments and holds records shooting against able-bodied archers.

Disabled archers have done well in international competitions as well. For example, Narohli Fairhall, a female competitor in a wheelchair from New Zealand won a gold medal in the 1982 Commonwealth Games and finished sixth in the women's archery competition in the 1984 Los Angeles Olympic Games.

Competitions

In the United States, many disabled archers compete on an equal basis with other archers in local and state archery competitions and hold memberships in the National Archery Association. In addition, disability organizations arrange competitions in which archers are grouped according to type and degree of impairment and functional ability.

In competitions for wheelchair users, men's and women's rounds are shot separately. Separate competitions are held in each round for those who use compound bows as adapted equipment. All other competitors use recurve bows.

In novice rounds for first-year competitors, archers shoot 36 arrows each from 50 and 30 meters at a 122-cm target. Those with more than one year's experience may compete in the short metric round, the advanced metric round or the FITA round.

The short metric is 36 arrows at 50 and 30 meters at an 80-cm target face. The advanced metric is 70, 50 and 30 meters for men and 60, 50 and 30 meters for women. The FITA round is the Olympic medal event: for the men's round, 36 arrows each at 90, 70, 50 and 30 meters; for the women's round, 36 arrows each at 70, 60, 50 and 30 meters.

Boys and girls who use wheelchairs compete under the aegis of the National Wheelchair Athletic Association. They shoot the same rounds as their able-bodied counterparts, who compete under the National Archery Association's Junior Olympic Archery Development Program.

Equipment, Rules and Training

Many types of bows and arrows are used in archery. Two important bow-selection factors are bow weight and the number of pounds necessary to bring it to full draw. Bow strength is measured in pounds; heavier bows are necessary to shoot longer distances.

For target shooting, most men use bows that average 35- to 45-pound pull; women usually select bows that require a somewhat lesser pull.

Beginning archers should not select a bow with too heavy a pull, since a bow with a too-heavy draw weight will slow development of good form. Also, they should practice within 20 meters of the target. Many beginning archers spend too much energy and concentration trying to pull the bow and aiming rather than concentrating on good overall technique.

Accommodations

Most archers with disabilities shoot from the same distance and in the same rounds as able-bodied archers. However, some modifications are made in special competitions. For example, persons with reduced power in arms and hands shoot in

the women's round or the mini round, where distances are shorter. In some cases, fewer arrows are fired during an official round. Time to complete a round is extended for classes in which more-severely disabled archers compete.

Devices such as camera tripods enable archers with balance and strength impairments to steady the bow and make vertical and horizontal aiming adjustments. If assistance is needed in holding the bow, a special cuff can be used.

Release aids have been developed that allow persons with flaccid fingers to pull and release bowstrings by pressing a trigger mechanism against their jaws or cheeks.

Most wheelchair archers place the wheelchair at a 90-degree angle to the target; some persons with upper-body impairment due to cerebral palsy may need to modify this position slightly. A proper seating position provides optimal balance when aiming the bow in a straight-arm position toward the target. People with cervical spine injuries may use a belt to secure their seating balance. By moving the body as close to the target side of the chair as possible, the archer can relax and lean against the back of the chair so that the bowstring does not touch the wheel of the chair. Wheelchair archers need to master the art of relaxing against the chair back without resting an arm on any part of the frame or push handle.

Archery is an increasingly popular sport among visually disabled persons, who improve kinesthetic and auditory skills with practice and enjoy the sense of accomplishment that comes with hitting the bull's-eye with regularity. Sound devices, some as simple as a radio placed behind the target, and photoelectric devices help the visually disabled archer line up the arrow with the target.

Lights can be used to signal time to fire (green to begin and red to cease) when archers with auditory impairments participate in competitions. A good safety precaution is to place hearing-impaired archers at the end of the firing line so that everyone else is easily within their line of vision.

"Disabled people should try archery—many do! It's a fascinating though difficult sport that requires long and disciplined training, and above all, hours of practice. It can take years to achieve competitive-level skills, but the personal satisfaction and rewards are well worth it."[3]

Conny Lindell *(Amputee)*
Editor of Swedish
Handicapped Sports Journal

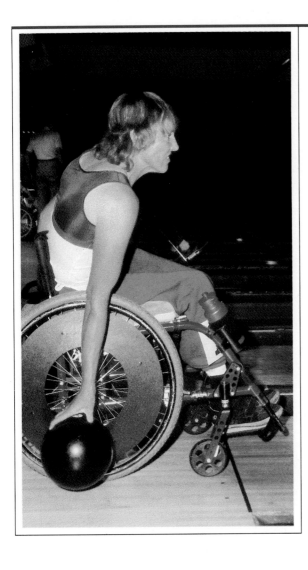

Bowling

Bowling is an important social activity as well as a demanding and exciting sport in which strong feelings of camaraderie develop among bowlers and spectators. The bowler has to think, judge, concentrate and interact with others while developing the physical skills the sport demands. As such, bowling is often a major motivating factor in getting newly disabled individuals out of the house and back into society.

Bowling has ancient origins in early Germany and ancient Egypt. By the Middle Ages, it had developed into a popular sport in Germany, similar to modern-day bowling. The game spread through the lowlands of Europe and was brought to the United States by the Dutch. The exact date is not known, but the first printed mention of the game was made by Washington Irving in "The Legend of Sleepy Hollow."

Despite the game's ancient origins in Europe, the United States pioneered bowling for blind people. It

has become an immensely popular sport among visually impaired people, who participate in bowling more than any other single sport.

No other sport combines competition and social interaction as successfully as bowling. Almost every bowling establishment has a coffee shop, and many have bars and excellent restaurants. Bowling establishments are usually open all day and often well into the night, making it possible for people to drop in to bowl at almost any time.

In bowling, each player, whether able-bodied or disabled, develops a personal scoring handicap. The handicap is the mean difference between an individual's scores obtained in competitions and the league's established standard. In essence, the bowler always competes against this personal handicap, making it possible for teams consisting of individuals of differing abilities, disabled and able-bodied, to compete equitably against each other.

There are other reasons why bowling is such a good sport for people with disabilities. The game offers those with and without impairments opportunities to enjoy a group and family activity together. In addition, most sports have a pattern of action-reaction in which players must react to other players' actions or performance. However, in bowling, the player determines his or her own technique and standards. Results are immediate—the bowling score provides instant feedback. This may well explain why so many people are challenged by the sport and find the competitive environment so rewarding.

"The act of competition is essential to the total development of any person, and that involvement in individual and team sporting events can teach a person humility and pride and instill a sense of self-worth and respect for others."[4]

National Association of Sports
for Cerebral Palsy

Accommodations and Technique

As in any sport, learning to bowl takes time and effort. The bowler learns to maintain balance and to coordinate muscles and joints to new motions associated with the game. With practice, persons with leg amputations who walk with prostheses usually learn to bowl with few modifications to style or technique. Other bowlers with mobility impairments but good upper-arm strength either bowl from a stationary position at the foul line, use a stepping approach or bowl from a wheelchair.

For wheelchair bowlers with limited arm strength, tubelike ramps can be used to guide the bowling ball. The bowler wheels into place on the approach to the lane, and the ramp is positioned on or beneath the arms of the chair and secured if necessary. The skill is in the bowler's ability to aim the ramp, since the slightest change in position can alter the direction of the roll and ultimate pin fall. Assistance can be provided to bowlers who cannot physically move the ramp. Pressure to set the ball in motion and the angle of the ramp determine ball speed; any part of the body can be used to set the ball in motion.

Bowlers who are able to stand but have difficulty holding the ball may use a special ball with handles on springs that retract when the ball is released. Pushing devices that cradle the ball, much like a shuffleboard stick, also can be used. Some bowlers initiate ball movement from prone positions on mattresses, stretchers or low gurneys. Any technique that gets results is permitted and encouraged.

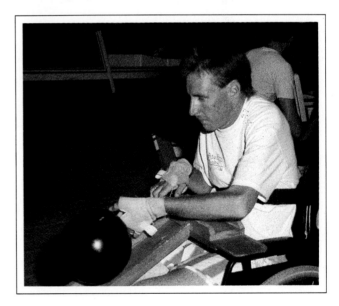

Blind and Visually Impaired Bowlers

In competitions, blind and visually impaired bowlers are classified according to their degree of visual impairment. All bowlers, including those with visual impairments, make constant adjustments according to feedback about their success in hitting the pins. During league games, sighted spotters provide this feedback by explaining which pin or combination of pins is left standing.

All lanes can be equipped with portable handrails so that visually impaired bowlers can determine the direction to move for the correct distance and approach. A narrow strip of rubber-backed carpet, about 10 inches wide by 12 feet long, can be used for the same purposes. It can be picked up if it is in the way of other bowlers and easily carried from one lane to another. Often, no special accommodation is needed—some blind bowlers orient themselves by using the ball-return channel or support structure as a guide.

Technology is making the sport more accessible to blind bowlers. The Telephone Pioneers of America have developed devices that allow visually impaired bowlers to bowl more independently. For example, the Pioneers developed an electronic board that allows bowlers to feel the position of remaining pins with their fingers. Using this device, blind bowlers can formulate a throwing strategy without having to rely on information provided by sighted companions.

Golf

Golf's ancient origins go back to various *club-and-ball* games reported in Roman times, medieval France and the Netherlands. However, the modern game comes from Scotland, where four centuries ago it survived legal prohibition enacted because its popularity posed a threat to the warlike and useful sport of archery.

Golf is a recreational and competitive activity in which individuals with disabling conditions participate together in special programs or right along with able-bodied partners. Players use a variety of clubs to propel a small ball around well-tended golf courses made challenging by obstacles such as sand bunkers, small ponds and rough ground. The aim is to *hole out* by using the smallest possible number of strokes to complete the course, which consists of 9 or 18 holes.

Almost everyone can play golf; success depends upon the power and precision of the golfer's swing when hitting the ball. According to Peter Longo, a world-class trick shot artist and author of *Challenge Golf* video tapes, "The golf swing can be adjusted to fit any need, and all the action is done from a standstill. Golf is the perfect game for . . . [many] disabled person[s]."[5]

Highly competitive tournaments have been held for a number of years for golfers with amputations, spinal cord-related disabilities and visual impairments. However, many golfers with disabling conditions play regularly with able-bodied friends and opponents. In fact, several individuals with disabling conditions—arm and leg amputees and paraplegics— have both taught and toured professionally.

One paraplegic pro plays with a swivel seat on his golf cart. He drives and hits from fairway and rough while sitting in his golf cart. The cart is equipped with a special seat that swings to the side, allowing him to address the ball from a quasi-standing position. When on greens or in traps, he leaves his cart, using a Canadian crutch, and plays the ball with a long-handled putter or wedge. Despite his disability, he drives well over 250 yards and scores consistently in the low 70s—a good score for any golfer. Another professional, a single-armed amputee, specializes in trick shots of all types. Two-armed golfers consistently are amazed at the power and accuracy of his one-arm swing.

Amputees use commonsense accommodations in order to play successfully, safely and with personal satisfaction any place, any time and with anyone.

One Arm By adjusting grip and arm position for maximum power and efficiency, the one-armed player makes optimal use of the nondisabled arm, hand, shoulder and leg action to produce a controlled golf swing. In recent years, a number of prosthetic arms equipped with adaptations designed for golf have become popular. Some golfers prefer the prosthetic arm because it adds stability and power by incorporating the disabled arm into the swing. Others find the one-armed swing more natural and comfortable. As always, with experimentation each person can find the approach that works best.

One Leg Because the full range of motion and power in arms and upper body is completely available, the one-legged golfer is almost on equal terms with two-legged opponents. The key to success is learning to retain balance while maximizing hip action and follow-through in the swing. Some one-legged players develop excellent balance skills without any aids. Others use a prosthetic leg and, with practice, achieve a virtually normal swing. Recent advancements in the design of prosthetic limbs greatly enhance the possibility of developing smooth and natural movements.

Chair Golf Many paraplegics, stroke patients and double-leg amputees play golf seated in a chair equipped with a seat belt to hold the body in a secure position. The seated golfer makes full use of arms, hands and shoulder motions to accomplish an effective, powerful and controlled golf swing. Most chair players find that a sport wheelchair (without arms) or a motorized golf cart with a seat that swings to the side of the cart is the best apparatus for playing golf. Sitting sideways in the golf-cart seat works if a rotating seat is not available.

Visually impaired golfers play with

winners often achieve total scores around 180.

Golf's greatest attribute, however, may be its recreational value. Given the use of scoring handicaps in golf, individuals with disabling conditions compete on equal terms with able-bodied golfers. On the course, friendships are developed and enhanced and business and social contacts are expanded while players have fun getting exercise and fresh air out-of-doors. These qualities are important to everyone, including those with disabling conditions. The many excellent golfing opportunities available to disabled individuals should be more widely used!

sighted partners who serve as their eyes, providing basic information—distance, direction, wind conditions, course conditions, location of traps and other obstacles. The blind golfer also receives assistance lining up and addressing the ball. On the green, verbal information is provided about the green—how it breaks, and the distance to the cup. To assist with putting, fellow golfers often reinforce this information by tapping a club or the flagstick in the hole.

In most tournament competitions involving blind and visually impaired golfers, two 18-hole rounds (36 holes) are played rather than the conventional 72 holes. National tournament

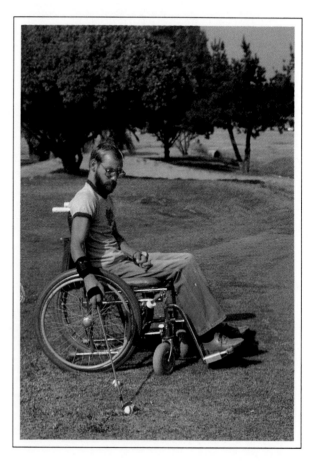

Gymnastics

Gymnastic performance as an entertainment, recreation and competitive athletic activity has ancient origins. Although the exact origin of gymnastics as a form of exercise is unknown, the histories of ancient China, India, Egypt, Greece and Rome all describe gymnastic activities as part of training and educating young people for citizenship and warfare. Tumbling and human pyramid-building are depicted in prehistoric drawings and carvings, and tumblers, acrobats, jugglers and rope dancers are mentioned frequently in ancient records.

Today, gymnastics is a highly competitive sport among young men and women. It requires superb conditioning, strength, skill and personal discipline. And, unlike most sports, the emphasis in gymnastics is on good form, in which preciseness of position, movement, correct posture and body mechanics are an integral part of every exercise. Style, which is closely related to good form, is a more elusive and intangible quality that conveys the impression of poise and confidence. Style distinguishes the champion performer from the merely competent.

Although no special competitive gymnastic opportunities are provided for disabled individuals other than for those with visual impairments, many individual success stories document accomplishments by disabled persons in regular programs:

- A senior-high-school boy, post-polio, was a two-time rope-climbing champion, setting a record in his senior year that stood for 10 years. The only time he was out of braces was when he practiced or competed.
- A former captain of the University of West Virginia gymnastics team successfully competed and

led the team despite the loss of his right leg at hip level in an automobile accident.

- At least two high school gymnasts have won still-ring championships, although each had lost a leg above mid-thigh level.
- Another post-polio athlete with an extremely atrophied left leg was an outstanding high school and YMCA gymnast, especially in all-around competition.

Several outstanding gymnasts with visual impairments have competed against able-bodied athletes at interscholastic and intercollegiate levels without any accommodations or modifications of rules. To encourage full participation, schools and organizations sponsoring gymnastics programs must be sure they are open to everyone and make individuals with disabling conditions aware of opportunities to participate.

Organized competitions for persons with visual impairments are made available through the United States Association for Blind Athletes (USABA). Events include floor exercise, balance beam, uneven bars, vaulting and all-around. USABA also offers a junior program that emphasizes developmental, noncompetitive personal fitness and basic gymnastic skills.

Three classes based on degree of visual impairment and four ability classes are recognized. In general, gymnasts may advance an ability level at any time and may compete in different events at different levels of ability.

As in gymnastics programs involving able-bodied individuals, the USABA program emphasizes competition. Preparation for competitive programs of this type involves regular and rigorous training, sacrifice

and high levels of personal fitness—muscular strength and endurance, flexibility and cardiovascular endurance. Speed, balance, agility, coordination and timing are other important physical requisites.

Serious gymnasts are daring, responsive to personal challenges and willing to explore the limits of their potential. Those traits are even more important for individuals who cannot see the apparatus on which they are performing or the areas in which they are to land. Therefore, *body sense* is especially important—the ability to know exactly what the body is doing and where it is at all times.

Increased awareness and exposure to gymnastics by disabled individuals and those who conduct gymnastics programs should lead to expanded opportunities for participation. By expressing interest in high school, university or community classes, disabled students can begin the process of making training in gymnastics available to more people with disabilities. Don't be reluctant to express your interest; you may find many others who share your enthusiasm!

Martial Arts

The martial arts include self-defense activities such as judo, tae kwon do and karate. Judo, which was developed in Japan in the nineteenth century, was introduced to the United States in the early 1900s. Today, it is a sport of worldwide popularity with over eight million participants. In the United States, judo enthusiasts and practitioners of other recently introduced martial arts are ardent advocates for their sport.

Concentration, continual practice and discipline are required of trainees, whose level of competence is signified by colored belts—white signifies beginners; black, highly skilled practitioners. Many martial arts programs emphasize life skills, maintaining that competence in martial arts leads to better overall fitness, concentration and self-confidence.

Competitions in judo for persons with disabilities are held in six classes that are determined solely by weight. Bouts last five minutes; scoring is based either on throwing or grappling techniques.

Classes have been held for wheel-chair users in several university and community programs. Instructors are usually individuals with a great deal of background and experience in martial arts. A number of individuals with disabilities have attained high levels of competence in one or more of the martial arts. Some have gained status through award and recognition programs, and some now teach martial arts to able-bodied and disabled students.

Martial arts classes with instructors who have disabling conditions have been successful components of rehabilitation programs in some hospitals and clinics. The disabled instructor serves as a role model for newly disabled patients, an extremely important function. Although physical gains from active participation in martial arts are not difficult to predict or see, the greatest gains may be psychological and emotional as participants develop self-confidence and esteem.

Shooting

Civic shooting festivals have been held in some northern European cities since the sixteenth century. Modern interest in target shooting, however, dates from the second half of the nineteenth century when technical advances in the manufacture of firearms led to much more accurate weapons.

Shooting disciplines differ as to the distance, form and nature of the target, the firearm and ammunition used, the position of the person shooting and the timing and number of shots fired. Shooting includes trap and skeet shooting, silhouette shooting, shooting with air rifles, and pistols, shooting with small- and large-bore rifles and hunting. Some events test pure marksmanship; others simulate hunting or combat in a highly stylized form.

Shooting is essentially a sport for the individual; scoring for team matches usually aggregates individual team member scores. Disabled and able-bodied people often compete and practice under similar conditions. As shooting becomes more popular and the demand for participation increases, more shooting ranges will become accessible to persons with physical disabilities.

Most disabled shooting events use the air rifle, air pistol or BB gun to shoot at a fixed target. In international competitions, male and female athletes compete in several disability classes.

In air rifle matches, prone, kneeling and sitting positions are used. When in the sitting position, the shooter rests both elbows on a table while shooting. When kneeling, the shooter rests one elbow on a table. When in the prone position, both elbows must rest on the floor. The sum of scores made in each of these three positions yields an aggregate score, which constitutes a medal event.

Technique

When shooting air guns, it is comparatively easy to find a place to practice. Distance is short, 10 meters, so it is possible to practice in a home basement or other safe area.

The expert marksperson must master basic safety precautions and certain fundamentals. Safety requires that the rifle or pistol always be pointed in a safe direction and treated as though it were loaded and the dangerous weapon that it is.

Shooting fundamentals start with a good shooting position—holding the rifle steady using proper support and balance and using bone and muscle structure to advantage and to compensate for disability. Next, the front and rear sights (markers on the weapon that show where the barrel is pointed) must be aligned on the target. The alignment may vary slightly, depending on the number of shots to be fired and distance from the target. Careful squeezing of the trigger while controlling breathing and consistent follow-through complete the cycle.

The sport is demanding regardless of the form of shooting practiced; to become skilled, body and mind must be trained to work together with great discipline and control. An initial practice session will demonstrate the time and patience required to develop precision—adjusting the weapon in hand, breathing properly, relaxing and concentrating, adjusting posture, aiming and firing. Step-by-step, the shooter learns to coordinate all parts of the body to achieve maximum precision.

Accommodations

By carefully selecting a weapon and shooting pattern, shooters can compensate for functional disabilities and minimize their effects on performances. The marksperson with good functional ability in the upper part of the body can usually participate in any form of shooting.

Possible accommodations include special cloth or leather grips, special firing mechanisms or help with loading the weapon and replacing targets. Since each competitor has a distinctive shooting pattern, accommodations are individual. Beginners should try different firearms and patterns before deciding how to proceed.

A form of air rifle shooting in Sweden is *Electron* shooting for visually impaired participants. The optic sight is replaced by an acoustic sight so that competitors *hear* how close their aim is to the target. The nearer the aim to the bull's-eye, the higher the pitch of sound given out by the acoustic sight. Precision is very high. The biathlon, which combines cross-country skiing with electron shooting, is a popular two-sport event in Sweden.

"Shooting is a sport well suited to many disabled people. It has the added advantage of being a sport where disabled and able-bodied can train and compete on equal terms."[6]

*Gregor Bonderud (Spinal Cord Injury)
Swedish Silver Medal Winner in
Shooting, 1984*

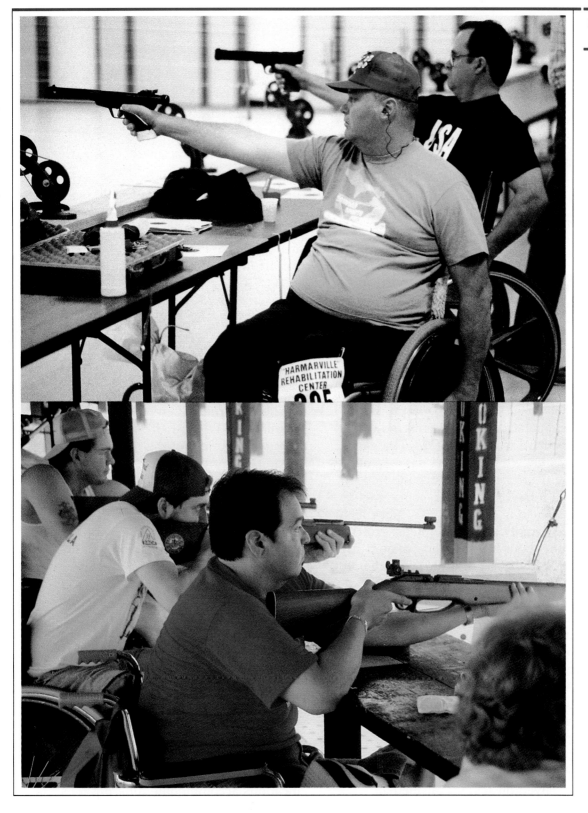

Wheelchair Racquetball

Racquetball developed as a variation on paddleball when, in the 1940s and 1950s, paddleball players decided that the game could be improved by using a strung racquet instead of the standard wooden paddle. The game was known by various names until the name *racquetball* was adopted when the first national tournament was held in the late 1960s. Racquetball rapidly became popular, growing from about half a million players in the early 1970s to well over three million in the early 1980s.

The game is played with a short-handled racquet and a hollow, pressurized ball in an enclosed, four-wall playing court (rules also allow for play on one- and three-wall courts). As in tennis, squash, handball and paddleball, players score points by hitting shots that cannot be returned by opponents.

Racquetball is a new sport for individuals in wheelchairs. The game is played on regular racquetball courts, so participation has been limited somewhat because of the lack of accessible courts and facilities.

The only rule difference between regular and wheelchair racquetball is that two bounces of the ball are permitted for participants in wheelchairs. Otherwise, all rules and strategies are identical. As it is for able-bodied participants, racquetball for wheelchair users can be a many-splendored thing—recreation, competition, fitness development and health maintenance.

Competitions at various levels—local to national—have been held for several years and are increasing in number each year. The American Amateur Racquetball Association (AARA) now promotes wheelchair racquetball. In 1986, for the first time, the wheelers' tournament was held at the same time as the AARA's singles tournament.

Commonsense variations and modifications accommodate differing

abilities, disabilities, strengths and weaknesses of participating individuals. For example, more than two bounces can be permitted, different serving approaches can be used, the number and combination of walls can be limited or less lively balls can be used.

One-wall racquetball using a gymnasium dividing door or the front wall of a regulation racquetball, handball or squash court provides excellent opportunities to learn and develop basic skills and for introductory and lead-up games.

Individuals with little or no background or experience in racquetball can develop skill rapidly, become proficient players and gain much personal satisfaction from participating. The future promises to be bright for racquetball as a recreational and competitive activity for growing numbers of wheelchair users.

Table Tennis

Although its origins are unclear, most reports indicate that table tennis first became popular in Great Britain and later spread across Europe before making its way across the Atlantic to find popularity in the United States in the 1920s. It is an important competitive sport in China and several other Asian countries, where skilled players sometimes become national heroes.

Table tennis is a favorite indoor activity because it is a keenly competitive game, requires little space and is inexpensive. It is also easy to learn. Even beginners can have great fun if not matched against a slamming master player. Furthermore, the game is good for you—table tennis improves concentration, reaction speed and coordination.

For these reasons, table tennis is a popular recreational activity, and many homes and most recreation centers feature tables where competitors use wooden paddles (usually covered with a rubber surface) to bat a small plastic ball back and forth across a center net. It is amazing that such an innocuous-appearing sport has so many enthusiastic adherents around the world!

Table tennis is one of the sports in which a person with a disability can play competitively against an able-bodied opponent. Many amputees and players in wheelchairs are members of table tennis clubs in their communities and play regularly in competitions against able-bodied persons.

Many disability organizations sponsor formal tournaments, and competitions are held at national and international levels. All disability categories are grouped in men's and women's singles and doubles events.

The difference in height between an able-bodied player who stands and a wheelchair player can be advantageous to the able-bodied player. To compensate, some serious wheelchair players use a special table tennis chair that is higher than usual. For most wheelchair users, a higher seat cushion solves the problem—as a test of proper height, adult players should be able to almost touch the net with their paddles.

If gripping the paddle is difficult, an elastic band or special bandage can be attached to the handle of the paddle and locked around the hand with a Velcro band.

Wheelchair play requires a lot of practice because it is not easy to play and maneuver the wheelchair at the same time. The player who cannot do both will end up overplayed and in a locked position. Since the wheelchair cannot move sideways and is difficult to move backwards with speed, the wheelchair player usually attempts to block the opponent's stroke at the table. Therefore, the wheelchair player's game is slightly more defensive than that of an able-bodied player.

Beginners can improve their game by concentrating on increasing accuracy and speed of shots. As in many sports, the beginning player can profit by getting pointers from experienced players.

Wheelchair Tennis

Tennis apparently derives from the ancient game of handball, which was first played in Greece. It later became a popular sport in Ireland and was a favorite pastime of the royal families of Europe for several centuries. The first form of the racquet used in modern tennis was a glove to protect the hand. Next, a small paddle was introduced to increase the striking area; the center of the paddle was eventually cut out and replaced with string. Today, no rules govern the size or shape of the modern tennis racquet, although rules do govern the size and weight of the tennis ball.

Wheelchair tennis is a relatively new sport in the United States—the first All-Comers competition was held in Southern California in 1976. Since then, the sport has become increasingly popular.

Wheelchair tennis is an attractive sport for many reasons. It is one of the sports that easily accommodates competition between able-bodied and wheelchair players, or with able-bodied and wheelchair players as partners. It combines the speed and quickness needed for basketball, the endurance needed for road racing and the delicate eye-hand coordination needed in skill sports such as archery and table tennis. Furthermore, the game can be played on any tennis court, and no playing area modifications are needed.

Tennis is a lifelong sport. Wheelchair tennis can be played for indoor or outdoor recreation or competition at virtually any age or skill level. It provides the satisfaction of performing a specialized motor skill, stimulates and improves circulation and breathing and exercises different muscle groups. Most important, wheelchair tennis offers opportunities to compete and participate with able-bodied friends and family.

PROFILE

Marilyn Hamilton

For 29 years, Marilyn Hamilton led an extraordinarily active life. She was a world traveler, beauty contest winner, skier and high school teacher. Her enthusiasm for life helped keep her going after she became paralyzed from the waist down after a hang gliding accident in 1979, when she "had to learn to do things in a different way." She learned to ski and, using a sit-ski, became a champion in the slalom, giant slalom and downhill divisions of the National Disabled Ski Championships in 1982.

Skiing was just the beginning. She held five national titles between 1981 and 1987 in the National Handicapped Ski Championships and was a member of the United States Disabled Ski Team in 1982 and 1987. She won a silver medal in the 1982 World Championships in Switzerland.

Hamilton's initial attempts to play tennis were frustrating because her conventional wheelchair didn't give her the mobility she wanted. So, working with medical experts, disabled people, and two friends who were manufacturing hang gliders, she helped design and manufacture the first "Quickie" lightweight wheelchair. That first chair led to a rapidly growing business called Motion Designs, which in turn led to Hamilton being named California Businesswoman of the Year in 1985. Using her Quickie chair, Hamilton became the Women's National Wheelchair Tennis Champion in 1982 and 1983.

An enormously successful woman, Hamilton has a number of tips for success. For example, she has this to say about giving and receiving: "Giving can be the easier of the two, especially for a giving person, but learning to receive is critical to achieving balance in your life. Drawing support from family and friends is vital in times of need; giving back in their times of need completes the cycle."

Since its inception as a recognized sport in 1976, wheelchair tennis has been the fastest growing and one of the most challenging and exciting of all wheelchair sports. In 1980 the National Foundation of Wheelchair Tennis was founded to foster development of wheelchair tennis. Today, more than 6,000 people in 32 states and 11 countries actively participate in the sport.

"[Tennis] not only helps my physical condition but it also really helped my head, and I think it can do the same for anybody else who wants it. What I've seen being in the chair for seven years now is that things couldn't be any better."[7]

Rick Slaughter (Paraplegic)
Wheelchair Tennis Player

Adaptive Equipment and Techniques

The game is easily modified to accommodate new players or players who lack strength, skill or mobility by altering the size of the court or eliminating certain types of shots. Such modifications are usually short-lived, however, as most players soon find themselves going after long balls and trying to make tough shots.

The simplest aid, as in other racquet sports, is a bandage that enables players to hold the racquet in a universal grip, allowing them to play forehand and backhand strokes without having to change grip. The bandage is applied in the shape of an "8" to hold the racquet firmly to the hand and wrist.

A lot of practice is needed to learn to control the game and the wheelchair at the same time. However, the light sports wheelchairs introduced in recent years make it easier than one might expect. The chair should sit low enough so the wheels can be turned about 90 to 120 degrees without leaning forward.

Competition and Player Eligibility

Wheelchair tennis can be played by anyone, regardless of age or disability. The only requirement for formal competition is that the player have a permanent disability that makes him or her unable to play ordinary tennis. The type of disability makes no difference.

For competitions, there are five classes for men and three for women. There is also an open junior division

and a class for quadriplegic players who need some aid in holding the racquet.

Players can choose to play in any division when taking up the sport. After winning two major tournaments in one year, the player must advance to the next division.

The Grand Prix Circuit, a series of national championship tournaments that exemplify the sport at its finest, was created in 1981. In 1984 the circuit became known as the Everest & Jennings Grand Prix Circuit. The 1987 circuit included 15 tournaments throughout the United States, 5 of which were National Championships. In 1987 the Seventh Annual United States Open Wheelchair Tennis Championship was presented by the Paralyzed Veterans of America. It boasted a draw of players from the United States, Brazil, Canada, Japan, Great Britain, Mexico, West Germany, Australia, Israel, France, Holland and New Zealand.

Rules and Strategy

The rules of tennis as set forth by the United States Lawn Tennis Association apply to wheelchair tennis, with one major exception—the wheelchair tennis player is allowed two bounces. The first bounce must land inside the court boundaries; the second may land anywhere. Although two bounces are allowed to make it easier to reach dead balls or short balls, most top players allow only one bounce.

The game of tennis breaks down to three basic components: racquet control, mobility and strategy. Strength in one area helps compensate for weakness in another. For example, a player who is slow but can place the ball accurately with just the right amount of spin will do well against the faster player who gets to the ball but hits it erratically.

Although height is not a great advantage in wheelchair tennis, quickness is. The more wheel turned with each push, the quicker the player can move and turn.

Technique

The grips and strokes used in wheelchair tennis are essentially those used in tennis. Players move with the racquet in hand, holding it in the forehand grip and using the fingers to turn the rim of the wheelchair. At higher speeds, the hand propels the rim while the thumb rests on the top side of the handle. Since this damages the handle of the racquet, players frequently cover the wheelchair rim with the same tape that is used on the racquet handle.

It is important to play with the racquet in hand at all times. It slows the game to hit a ball, put the racquet between the legs or on the lap, move, pick up the racquet and return the next ball. Some players prefer a racquet with a thin handle, which makes it easier to manage the racquet and the wheelchair rim at the same time.

Weightlifting

According to legend, Milo, a great Grecian athlete of the sixth century, developed tremendous strength by repeatedly lifting a calf while it grew to maturity. Milo then exhibited his great strength by carrying a live ox around the course at the Olympic stadium.

Numerous records through the ages describe trials of strength involving lifting, but weightlifting in its present form using barbells began in Western Europe in the nineteenth century, when professional strongmen appeared in music halls and circuses. Today, weightlifting is an important competitive sport, and weight training has become an essential component of training for gymnasts, swimmers, basketball players and other athletes.

Training

Because few modern sports overload the muscles with heavy resistance, weight training is needed to build strength and overall fitness.

Simply stated, the overload principle means that muscles are forced to do something they are not accustomed to doing. Methods of overloading include increasing weights, repetitions or sets; decreasing rest periods; and increasing speed of movements or the speed with which the entire set is performed. Much training takes place on Nautilus or other resistance machines, which are found in virtually every health, racquet and gym facility in the United States.

Competitions

Competitive weightlifting requires great physical strength developed through rigorous training. Classifications for men and women are categorized by both body weight and medical classification; all major disability groups offer formal weightlifting competitions which culminate every four years in Paralympic competitions. Weighing in takes place before the competition, with no prosthesis. Weight classifications for amputees are determined by adding weight factors based on the ratio of degree of amputation to body weight.

In disabled weightlifting competitions, barbells are lifted from a position 1 inch off the chest in the bench press, the only recognized position for persons with lower body impairments. The lifter lies supine on a horizontal bench, with head, shoulders, buttocks and legs remaining in contact with the bench throughout the lift. A legal lift occurs when the pressing movement is continuous, with even arm extension. The press is completed when the lifter is motionless with the barbell under control at arm's length.

When lifting free weights, spotters should always be used to ensure safety.

PROFILE

Kristoffer Huleki

Kristoffer Huleki, a Swedish weightlifter, may be the strongest man in the world for his class. He has lifted three times his body weight and holds the world record for able-bodied weightlifting for his weight class. Although he is a wheelchair user who was disabled by polio as a child, Huleki has set all of his records in able-bodied competitions. However, he also participates regularly in the Paralympics.

Huleki's response to the challenge of weightlifting was once inhibited by difficulty controlling his nerves. At a competition in 1981, despite his prowess in his sport, he was unable to complete one good lift. With practice and perseverance, however, Huleki triumphed over his nerve problem. At the 1986 European Championships, he won the international gold medal in his class. In the 1987 World Championships in Paris, he broke the European record in the 165-pound class by lifting 462 pounds and received a gold medal.

Although training and competing are Huleki's primary activities, he takes the time to support the Swedish organization, Sports Against Apartheid. He says that sport has been crucial in his development: "Sport has formed me totally. It has been hard work, but it has given me so much."

Wrestling

Wrestling is one of the most basic forms of competition between individuals. References to wrestling can be traced back into prehistory through ancient Greece, Egypt, Mesopotamia and India.

Today, it is an important competitive sport at the high school and college level for visually impaired athletes, who have done well at both interscholastic and intercollegiate wrestling competitions. To date, other disability groups have not sponsored wrestling competitions.

Wrestling has long been a basic activity in state schools for visually impaired students who compete against each other and against teams of sighted wrestlers. Often, as many as 50 visually impaired wrestlers place in state high school meets across the United States.

Some of these same individuals have wrestled successfully at the collegiate level. During the 1984 U.S. Olympic Festival in North Carolina, a team of visually impaired wrestlers

representing the United States Association for Blind Athletes (USABA) competed against a team of hearing-impaired wrestlers representing the American Athletic Association for the Deaf (AAAD). All wrestlers competed in both Greco-Roman and catch-as-catch-can styles. Jim Mastro was the only USABA athlete who won matches, although most were hotly contested. This same Jim Mastro was an alternate member of the 1976 U.S. Olympic wrestling team that competed in Montreal.

Wrestling is included in the national games of USABA. At the international level, wrestling is an exhibition event, since the sport is not as developed or as popular throughout the world as it is in North America.

Basically, the rules are identical for visually impaired and sighted athletes except that if, when in a standing position, wrestlers do not *lock*, no move can be made to go behind an opponent. If such a move is made, action is stopped, the offender is warned, and action is reinstated. If wrestlers are *locked*, then moves to the rear of an opponent are legal. This rule change applies whether a visually impaired wrestler is competing against a sighted or another visually impaired opponent.

Portions of this chapter were taken from materials or comments provided by Gregor Bonderud, Sven Briefe, Kay Ellis, John Högberg, Conny Lindell, Peter Longo, Brad Parks, Julian Stein and Robert Szyman.

REFERENCES

[1] Engström, G. and Augustsson, L. (eds.). *Kom Igen* (Malmö, Sweden: Liber Förlag, 1985), p. 118.

[2] Stein, J. (ed.). *Values of Physical Education, Recreation, and Sports for All* (Reston, VA: American Alliance for Health, Physical Education, Recreation and Dance, Unit on Programs for the Handicapped), pp. 25–26.

[3] Engström, op. cit. p. 68.

[4] National Association of Sports for Cerebral Palsy. From "Statement of Philosophy," *Classification and Sport Rules Manual* (New York, 1983), p. 5.

[5] Longo, P. *Challenge Gold—Instruction for Physically Handicapped* (Peter Longo, P.O. Box 821, Bensenville, IL 60106).

[6] Engström, op. cit. p. 60

[7] United States Olympic Foundation. *Images of Excellence* (Boulder, CO: Videotape prepared by United States Olympic Committee, Committee on Sports for the Disabled, February 8, 1988).

CHAPTER
3
OUTDOOR SPORT and RECREATION

Introduction

Outdoor sport and recreational activities are favorite pastimes in North America and Europe. For many, time spent outdoors away from crowds of people restores the soul and rekindles the spirit. Exercise refreshes the body, and the challenge of canoeing, horseback riding, hiking or wilderness adventure, despite a disability, stimulates the mind and reinforces the sense of being one with nature.

People with disabilities enjoy the out-of-doors as much as anybody else. Senses are sharpened as people experience nature by paddling a canoe down a river or tramping through woods; smelling and touching stones, trees and vegetation; hearing sounds of the wind in the trees, the animals beside the path and the steps of companions on the trail; and feeling the surface of rocks or water underfoot and the weather on the skin.

Many outdoor activities are pursued by people with disabilities. Hunting, fishing, picnicking, bird watching and camping, for example, are favorite pastimes. As disabled people seek more outdoor opportunities, the staff of national, state and local parks and recreational areas have become more aware of the needs of visitors with disabilities. As a result, trails, paths and park facilities are becoming more accessible.

Improved equipment also makes a difference. For example, hikers using lightweight wheelchairs with knobby tires now traverse paths and even travel up mountain trails previously considered inaccessible by wheelchair users.

Publications such as *Accent on Living, Disabled Outdoors, Sports 'n Spokes* and numerous newsletters feature outdoor recreational activities pursued by people with disabilities. Travel information can be obtained from *The Itinerary*, a magazine specializing in travel for disabled people.

Readers should be aware that the wide range of types, costs and modifications available for recreational

vehicles makes discovering the countryside and accessing natural areas easier now than ever before. In addition, all-terrain vehicles (ATVs) and snowmobiles make some activities, such as hunting, feasible for the first time for many people with impaired mobility.

The following pages describe several outdoor activities. Canoeing and kayaking are especially attractive to people with mobility impairments because water solves many mobility problems. People with good upper-arm muscular strength and endurance are able to canoe and kayak with relative ease, bringing along their lightweight wheelchairs on lengthy trips. In fact, canoeists have packed two lightweight, foldable wheelchairs along with the necessary camping gear into a single canoe.

Other sections describe adventure trips, hiking, cycling, horseback riding and orienteering. A final section describes recreational travel opportunities. As with many activities described in this book, strong interest, ingenuity and determination make all the difference.

"To climb a mountain and stand on top and breathe high and clean air, to glide underwater with a sensation of weightlessness, to have a good stretch on skis or go down a mountainside, to go quietly across water in a canoe in the wilderness, to walk with a heavy load on your back or to cook your food over an open fire is a freedom everybody has a right to enjoy."[1]

Annika Larsen *(Visually Impaired)*
Swedish Skier, Diver, General Outdoorswoman

Canoeing, Kayaking and Rafting

The canoe is one of the oldest means of transportation we know—the first canoe was probably made from a hollow log. In a canoe, one can experience the countryside, rivers and lakes in new ways, intensely and closely. An investment in a canoe or kayak is an investment in joy, peace and fitness in spring, summer and autumn. While moving slowly through whispering trees and along inviting beaches or gliding silently over rocks, a canoeist experiences both the wonder of life and the rewards of camaraderie with fellow canoeists.

Canoeing is an ideal sport for persons with mobility impairments. The canoe is a surprisingly stable craft, especially when the operator sits below water level.

Canoeing is all about the interplay among muscles, paddles, canoes and waves. Respect for water and safety precautions—use of life jackets and man-overboard drills—are fundamental elements of the sport, even though modern canoes do not sink even if filled with water. Good swimming ability is recommended for any water activity, and canoeing is no exception. Although canoeing is primarily considered a recreational activity, racing canoeists relish the challenge and excitement of highly charged competitive races across lakes and down white-water rapids.

Both the United States and Sweden offer fantastic canoeing country. Sweden has 100,000 lakes and a

large, beautiful coastline and archipelago. Few countries offer such an El Dorado for a canoeist, except, perhaps, the United States—the Adirondacks, the Maine woods, the boundary waters between Ontario and Minnesota and countless rivers immediately come to mind.

Individuals with good upper-arm muscular strength, trunk balance and endurance manage canoes with only minor additional adaptations; others can participate with adaptations as paddlers or as riders, navigators, storytellers and sometimes cooks. Adaptations are rapidly evolving, including rowing machines to

facilitate indoor training and buoyant paddles that make paddling easier. The sport is new enough that most adaptations are still being developed in the backyards and shops of ardent canoeists. Such adaptations, when commercially available, are advertised in publications such as *Palaestra* and *Sports 'n Spokes*.

Although both canoeing and kayaking can be performed solo or in tandem, tandem arrangements are often preferred by people with disabilities. If a canoeist is visually impaired, a sighted partner can serve as eyes and steer the boat. If a canoeist is mobility impaired, the able-bodied partner

provides an extra margin of safety if an accident occurs and assists with camping chores and portaging over land areas between bodies of water.

"Canoes can be rather expensive, but it is difficult to find a better investment. A canoe can give you joy, serenity, fitness and fellowship in spring, summer and autumn. As you slowly move along the river banks between the murmuring trees, through canyons and mountains, you feel that life is wonderful, and conversations with paddling partners touch on the important things in life."[2]

Bernt Eklundh (One-Leg Amputee)
Swedish Canoeist

Canoeing

There are several distinct types of canoeing. *Flat-water canoeing,* the easiest form of canoeing, is associated with slow-moving rivers and lakes. *White-water canoeing,* a more exciting and difficult form of the sport, involves running rapids down rivers or paddling through high-standing waves.

Canoe touring primarily involves flat-water trips of at least two days, with overnight camping. One of the biggest physical challenges involved in a canoe trip is *portaging,* crossing ancient trails and land areas that separate rivers and lakes. Portaging provides new opportunities for co-operation—for example, a non-disabled person or a person who uses a wheelchair might team up with a person who is visually impaired or with a person with cerebral palsy. Together they navigate the rocks, roots and inclines that might prove insurmountable to each if attempted alone.

Canoe racing is enjoyed by more and more people each year as an alternative to running, bicycling or wheelchair racing. Its devotees depend largely on upper-body muscular strength and endurance, discipline and stamina. Other than their contribution to balance, the legs are not used at all.

Canoe racing is a well-established sport with many local and some national competitions. Classes established by the American Canoe Association are based on sex, weight and age. Classification consists of three categories, with competitors in each class ideally having different physical characteristics, paddling styles and equipment. To date, no disability classes have been established.

The first racing category, *slalom*, demands muscular strength and endurance, speed and precise timing. Boats used in slalom racing are compact and highly maneuverable, and long, straight paddles provide control.

The second category, *long-distance racing*, consists of races of at least 13 miles. These races, the marathons of canoeing, require strength and enormous endurance. The third category, *downriver* or *wildcat races* of 5 to 13 miles, often take place in choppy waters.

To develop strength and stamina, simple, lightweight exercise machines are available for use in the home. If properly used, they can help improve the canoeing stroke, stimulate cardiovascular/respiratory function and

strengthen arms and upper-body musculature.

Adapting a Canoe. The major concern in selecting and outfitting a canoe for people with mobility and balance impairments is stability. The second concern is often speed—the longer the canoe, the greater its potential speed. In addition, comparatively large canoes are desirable for tandem canoeing and carrying wheelchairs.

Although canoes come in different sizes and models, most are lightweight—a 17- to 18-foot canoe generally weighs 75 pounds or less. Most are easily transported and moved into the water and are large enough to carry gear and a wheelchair.

Accommodations to increase stability and individual comfort are available. An individual's center of gravity is controlled by lower-trunk muscles, which help hold the canoeist on the comparatively high seat of most canoes. Thus, lowering the seat is the best way to increase stability for those with impairments in the lower-trunk area. Depending on the construction of the canoe, a seat can be lowered by simply removing it and hanging it on four-inch bolts screwed into the gunwale or by riveting the seat to the sides of the canoe.

A sling seat developed by Wilderness Inquiry in Minnesota replaces the original canoe seat. Straps are attached to the gunwale, and the seat is tilted back as desired, lowering the hips (and raising the knees) to increase comfort and stability. At the time of this book's publication, the sling seat was not available commercially.

Another simple adaptation is an inexpensive black plastic seat back marketed by Coleman Canoe for fishermen who want to lean back while fishing. The seat clips onto the existing canoe seat, providing additional back support and stability for individuals with balance difficulties. A rod can be wrapped with padding and attached in front of the seat to provide a raised leg rest for the knees, which lowers the hips into a more stable position. Another simple adaptation involves installing a bean-bag chair in the bottom of the canoe—a cheap, durable and light-weight approach to stability and comfortable sitting.

A paddle wheel has been developed for people who lack muscular strength and endurance in their arms and hands. It is used like a hand-driven bicycle to provide power and balance for canoeists who are paralyzed in the upper body.

Canoeists with lower-trunk impairments should carry plenty of foam padding to protect against rubbing and pressure sores. In addition, most canoeists use their own wheelchair cushion to pad their seat while in the canoe.

Canoeing with Visual Impairments. Because it is very difficult, if not impossible, to stay on course without sight in open water, even if the direction of the wind is known, persons with visual impairments usually pair up with sighted canoeists. A double canoe is easier to handle than a

single canoe, and communication is easier, especially in a strong wind where the voice does not carry well. There should always be full agreement about the meaning of directions, because quick corrections are sometimes necessary.

Before attempting swiftly moving streams and rapids, canoeing pairs with one visually impaired member should practice extensively together, and the exact meaning of each command must be known and rehearsed in advance. For example, often the canoe must quickly move sideways to avoid rocks or to be in position to catch the current. The sighted person should be at the bow to watch for rocks and other obstacles such as floating logs.

Kayaking

As with canoeing, kayaking can take several forms. *White-water kayaking* involves twisting, turning and spinning through rapids of varying lengths and difficulties. A comparatively short, highly maneuverable kayak with no rudder is used for river kayaking.

Sea kayaking, which is comparable to flat-water canoeing, takes place on lakes, oceans and large bodies of water such as the Great Lakes and broad rivers. Longer, more stable and faster kayaks with a rudder attached to the stern are used. Only well-trained kayakers with experienced partners should attempt the open sea. A sudden sideways wash from a speedboat, large ship, rogue wave or unexpected large swell can easily capsize a small craft.

Kayaks originated with the Eskimo people. Kayaks are a variation of canoe design in which the kayaker's body and gear fit tightly through openings in the top to rest on the floor of the kayak, below water level. The design makes the kayaker feel part of the boat and the water, and thus creates an opportunity for a more efficient paddling pattern. Double-bladed paddles are used to propel the kayak. In the San Juan three-hole kayak, the third hole accommodates a lightweight wheelchair and sufficient gear for extended camping trips.

"For years some friends and I had a good deal at a swimming pool at the University of Colorado. It was called a kayaking course for the disabled. I was the token gimp, and my many "instructors" and I got to use the pool to run gates or practice Eskimo rolls or just horse around.

Then one day, this guy with a real fast wheelchair—you know, no brakes, no arm rests, cambered wheels, nine-position axle, tiny casters, damped forks, spoilers—well, this guy showed up with a borrowed boat, put a piece of packing foam in the bottom of the cockpit, braced his back against what looked like the side of an orange crate, and announced that he was ready to learn to kayak. His injury looked high to me, perhaps T2, perhaps too high for a sport that demands so much of the upper body. He didn't know or care. Now, he's a pretty fair kayaker. And he's not T2. He's C7,8."[4]

West Brownlow *(Spinal Cord Injury)*
Wheelchair Athlete

Kayaks come in different materials and designs. Most are made of fiberglass, plastic or Kevlar. Some are designed for speed and lack stability, while longer, more stable kayaks are best handled with a rudder. Many dealers allow customers to try several boats and paddles before making a purchase.

Few modifications to the kayak are needed to accommodate most disabilities, although some adjustments to seat and back support or bracing may be helpful for the person with a double leg amputation. Individuals-with amputations who kayak sometimes choose to strap their prosthesis in the kayak rather than to their body, since the prosthetic device could entrap its owner if the kayak capsized. For the same reason, a peg leg may be desirable.

Members of the *one-leg club* should be forewarned—salt water can be like glue. The stump must be washed before the prosthesis is attached again, so extra fresh water should be included with other gear.

"When I glide through the water in my canoe, when I feel the wind and waves and smell the forest air, I am part of nature. I discover even more of nature when we get on shore, set up camp and cook a meal. It is an overwhelming experience to be near a roaring waterfall, feeling the mist and spray of water on my face."[3]

Annika Larsen (Visually Impaired)
Swedish Outdoorswoman

"My most memorable experiences were paddling my first canoe, sleeping in a tent for the first time, being sat upon by a 200-pound blind man, drinking water from the lake and seeing all of those delicious berries just waiting to be eaten."[6]

Participant, Wilderness Inquiry
Adventure Trip

Adventure Experiences

Adventure experiences combine the physical challenge of confronting new outdoor environments with the psychological and emotional excitement of functioning within a group in a rugged and sometimes hostile environment. In July of 1986, 13 people of mixed abilities and disabilities made a 700-mile canoe trip through the remote wilderness of the northern Yukon and northwestern Alaska under the auspices of Wilderness Inquiry, an outdoor adventure program based in Minneapolis, Minnesota. Greg Lais, who led the group, describes the experience:

"We came together as strangers, found what each other's needs were, and melded as a team to meet those collective needs. Set against the backdrop of a wilderness environment indifferent to our existence, we realized our common human needs far outweighed our differences. In the process, we overcame our fear of the

Linda Phillips

Linda Phillips, a participant in several wilderness trips, has become a strong advocate for wilderness preservation. What is unusual is that Phillips is deaf and a high-level quadriplegic due to an automobile accident. Although Phillips is accompanied by a personal attendant, she participates in most activities, including the canoe tip test, a required safety procedure, and she swims regularly, using a life jacket.

Phillips' love of travel and of the outdoors led her to explore wilderness trips. Her first experience, a canoe trip through the boundary waters at the northeastern border of Minnesota and Canada, led to "overwhelming joy—the actual happening exceeded all expectation."

Each trip is a new experience for Phillips, who helps with the cooking and regularly finds she is able to do things she never thought possible. She is greatly admired for her gung-ho attitude and is proclaimed by her fellow travelers as a "fine companion."

bush and of ourselves. By the end of the trip, no distinctions were made between the physically disabled and nondisabled members of the group. These did not matter anymore."[5]

For those of us who lack the confidence to camp and travel alone in the great outdoors or the time to make the necessary preparations, organized camping and adventure trips may be the best approach. Several private organizations either provide experiences exclusively for people with disabilities or plan at least some of their trips and outings in a manner that makes disabled people welcome and comfortable members of the activity.

For example, a typical Wilderness Inquiry group might include two people in wheelchairs; two who are sensory impaired, blind or deaf; two who have some other disability but can walk on their own; and any number of able-bodied people.

Although people with many disabilities participate in adventure trips, certain health conditions may jeopardize a person's safe participation—for example, persons requiring assistance with transfers whose weight (more than approximately 190 pounds) makes it difficult or unsafe for others to carry them, persons with decubitus ulcers and those who need

"Outdoor adventure is a tool which empowers people to realize their full potential as human beings."[7]
Participant, Vinland National Center

daily attention by professional medical personnel. Wheelchair users regularly participate, although the weight of electric wheelchairs precludes their use. Persons who require much assistance in personal hygiene or who have special needs usually bring an attendant who is familiar with their care.

Trips take groups of people down long rivers and through the mazelike systems of interconnecting lakes in northern Minnesota, through the Allagash Wilderness in Maine, down the Current and Buffalo rivers in the Ozarks and the Rio Grande in Texas, into Alaska and the Canadian Shield country and even above the Arctic Circle. Wilderness Inquiry trips use canoes during summer and dogsleds during winter.

Another kind of outdoor experience is offered by the Breckenridge Outdoor Education Center, located on 38 acres in Breckenridge, Colorado.

Year-round programs are available for children and adults of all ages who have special needs and varying abilities. The programs and instructional courses, which range in length from one to ten days, offer hiking, horseback riding and fishing experiences.

Voyageur Outward Bound, one of the largest and best-known outdoor adventure organizations in the United States, has been offering integrated programs for physically disabled people since 1976. Canoeing and dog sledding are primary modes of transportation.

Equally tempting experiences are available from other organizations.

"People say, 'I didn't know I could do that. I didn't know I could catch a fish or paddle a kayak two miles.' "[8]

Shorty Powers (Paraplegic)
Participant in an
Independent Nature Trip

Hiking

Hiking, or *fell walking*, the European term for hiking through rough terrain, is a favorite outdoor activity that is more accessible today than ever before because of the availability of rugged, lightweight wheelchairs that can traverse rough terrain.

Good balance is needed for hiking to be an enjoyable and safe experience. Although hikers usually carry the heaviest items at the top of rucksacks to make uphill climbs easier, this loading makes balance more difficult. Visually disabled people and others who have difficulty with balance usually feel safer if heavier items, such as tents, are carried at the bottom of packs.

Persons with amputations can modify prostheses to make movement more comfortable or feasible. For example, crutches can be modified, or adjustable crutches can be used. A 12-inch basket attached to the bottom end of the crutch can stop it from sinking into the snow. When Sarah Doherty, an amputee, made her historic ascent of Mount Rainier in

1984, a special basket with a convex surface and spikes was created for her crutch so that it would not fill with snow and could be used to grip the surface. Some people with leg amputations use a special insert to reduce friction between the residual limb and the prosthesis. A foot assembly that provides motion in all planes can also be helpful, especially when climbing in mountainous areas.

Persons with vision, mobility, or balance impairments may prefer the company of others when walking in unfamiliar surroundings or over rough trails. Sometimes a helping hand is necessary. Because hiking paths are usually too narrow for side-by-side walking, it is often easier for a disabled person to follow companions around swamps, on slopes, and in brushwood, although such arrangements always are made to suit personal preferences and abilities. When hiking in varied terrain, a loose strap can be attached to the guide's rucksack, one end at the top and one at the bottom, like a handle. As the guide leads, the blind hiker can, by holding the strap, feel the ups and downs of the trail ahead.

Guides accompanying persons with visual disabilities describe obstructions and details of the trail ahead, such as large boulders, planks or logs serving as footbridges, or streams that must be jumped. When crossing narrow planks or streams, the guide usually should go first, followed closely by the blind person, who may choose to hold the strap on the guide's backpack for direction and balance. A wider stream should be crossed by holding hands and stepping carefully on the bottom of the stream to avoid boulders or other slippery spots.

Cycling

Man had known about the wheel for centuries before anyone thought about putting two of them in a line and holding them together with a frame. No one knows who thought of it first, but a design has survived of a crude wooden two-wheeler used shortly after the French Revolution. It is fitting that France should be the birthplace of the bicycle, because every year the French live in suspended animation during the three-week Tour de France road race. As many as 100,000 picnicking fans turn out to enjoy this annual world championship event.

Cycling is still a primary mode of transportation in some parts of the world, including the Netherlands and China. For most of Europe and the United States, however, cycling is primarily a recreational and racing sport.

Cycling is an exhilarating experience that gives a particular feeling of grace, speed, independence and mobility. This feeling is particularly pleasant for people with mobility difficulties and visual impairments. In addition, cycling is marvelous fitness training that is all the more pleasurable because it takes place out-of-doors and can be combined with other activities, such as touring the countryside and running errands.

A good cyclist combines athletic ability, extensive hard training, properly fitting equipment and smart riding. Smart riders *always* wear helmets—many serious biking accidents have resulted in head injuries that would have been prevented had a helmet been worn. The cycle should be as lightweight as possible, well maintained and lubricated. A lightweight frame with multiple gears and high-pressure tires is a good investment.

Cycling has many variations including tandem cycling with an experienced partner, a suitable arrangement for many persons with visual impairments or those who have difficulty balancing alone. Many people with

visual impairments race regularly in tandem races.

An offshoot of the standard two-wheel bicycle is the three-wheel tricycle used by both able-bodied and disabled individuals. The United States Cerebral Palsy Association offers competitive trike events for participants who have difficulty operating bicycles.

Most individuals with lower-limb amputation or paralysis who have strong upper-body and limb control can ride a hand-cycle trike. Hand cycles provide pleasurable outdoor activity and good exercise on the many bike paths that now crisscross most major cities and parks. Hand bikes can be used for transportation to work, for running errands and for racing.

Standard handlebars are replaced by a hand-cranked chainwheel and linkage attached to the front wheel to provide propulsion and a steering mechanism. For example, the *Trike 324*, designed and manufactured in Boston by Bill Warner, a paraplegic engineer, offers a 24-speed system suitable for many terrains, a cruising speed of 10 to 15 miles per hour, and sprinting speeds of 20 miles per hour. Braking is achieved by backpedaling with the hands. A number of other classy racing hand cycles are regularly advertised in *Sports 'n Spokes*.

Another alternative for the wheelchair user is a comparatively inexpensive, lightweight and durable hand-cycle unit that weighs about 17 pounds. A single wheel and hand pedals are attached to the front of a standard (preferably lightweight) wheelchair, allowing it to be pedaled

entirely by hand. With experience, the unit can be attached in less than 30 seconds. The cyclist can travel at speeds of 10 to 15 miles per hour, covering 3 to 5 miles at this speed with relative ease. Standard 3-speed and 5-speed models are readily available.

Racing

The United States Cerebral Palsy Athletic Association sponsors 1,500- and 5,000-meter tricycle and bicycle races. The United States Association for Blind Athletes sponsors 10- and 40-kilometer tandem and single races for men and women. National competitions are held by both organizations, and winners proceed to the international games.

In 1983 Dave Kiefer's *Ride Across America* established a handicapped world record by cycling across the country in just 17 days, 5 hours and 7 minutes. Kiefer's achievement is particularly noteworthy because he cycled using just one leg and exceeded his goal to "double" the able-bodied record of 9 days, 20 hours and 2 minutes set in 1983 by Lon Haldeman. Kiefer rode without a prosthesis with a team of six cyclists at an average speed of 20 miles per hour, or an average of 160 miles per day. He spent from 10 to 18 hours each day on the road.

Technique, Training and Conditioning

Preseason conditioning to develop endurance requires many miles of training, spinning at low gears. Pat

Pride, a coach of athletes with cerebral palsy, does not recommend pedaling at high gears; too much pushing results in knee strain and injuries. Fast spinning in lower gears produces better results. A quick cadence (pedaling speed) of around 70 revolutions per minute is the ticket to fast riding and better cardiovascular conditioning. In addition, legs get stronger, become less fatigued and move faster.[9]

Regular (biweekly) interval racing, in which the rider spins higher gears at a faster cadence than usual, is recommended for developing speed; too much interval riding, however, taxes the body and can cause sport-related injuries.

Schwinn has developed an indoor stationary bicycle exerciser for disabled individuals that operates on an air-displacement principle, providing a range of variable, measured work loads combined with cooling effects from its own wind-vane system. Arm levers and pedals work separately or in concert to allow simultaneous workout of upper and lower limbs.

Horseback Riding

Learning to ride a horse is a challenging activity that involves the entire body. Every muscle and joint is used, resulting initially in a sore body. However, with practice one can achieve improved musculature, balance and coordination. Many people with disabilities become excellent riders, and some take part in national and international competitions.

Horseback riding as recreation or physical therapy for those with disabilities is a fairly recent development. The first disabled person to undertake a therapeutic riding program was a Danish woman, Liz Hartel. She was a great competitive rider who contracted polio in the late 1940s. Although doctors told her that her riding days were finished, she began to ride again. The experience was so rewarding and the therapy so effective that she continued with a rigorous regimen of training and eventually won a silver medal in the 1952 Olympics in Helsinki.[10]

Her success caused some physicians in Europe to begin researching the health benefits of riding. This led to the development of training programs used today. Although the goal of most trainees is to have fun while learning to ride, the therapeutic benefits of horseback riding can be impressive.

Wendy Shugol, an accomplished sportswoman who competes internationally in horseback riding and swimming competitions, reports that

"Riding creates togetherness. Riders tend to gather at the stables even when they are not planning to ride, perhaps to care for their horse or to greet friends. What riders have in common is an interest and love for horses—it provides a bond for the friendships that develop."[11]

Ulla Ståhlberg
Swedish Pioneer in Disabled Riding

when she first gets on the horse, her muscles and her entire body are rigid from the effects of cerebral palsy. But after exercising the horse for a few minutes, her muscles begin to relax, and she can place her feet in the stirrups.

No one knows why riding has this effect on persons with cerebral palsy and other physical disorders. However, it is known that riding can improve balance and trunk control in all riders, that it improves mental alertness in autistic children and helps calm hyperactive children and brings a tremendous emotional lift to most disabled riders.

Most riding programs emphasize therapy and, to a more limited extent, competition. Often individuals who graduate from therapeutic programs have little opportunity to ride for fun and recreation unless they can afford to own their own horse—few commercial stables offer accessible facilities (accessible restrooms and parking, a mounting ramp, hard and smooth access to the riding facility). In addition, a suitable horse with a gentle temperament and a smooth, even gait is needed.

Accommodations

The individual with an amputation who rides needs few, if any, modifications to the bridle and reins unless use of the hands and arms is affected. Usually the saddle will not require changes, but handholds can be attached to make balancing easier and to make the reins easier to grasp. Although riding without a prosthesis does not necessarily upset the rider's

PROFILE

Wendy Shugol

Wendy Shugol, an international competitor in horseback riding and swimming, has cerebral palsy and severe diabetes. In addition to equestrian competition in dressage events, she competes in international 50-meter freestyle and 25-meter backstroke swimming events.

In 1982, as a member of a riding exhibition at the Fifth International Cerebral Palsy Games in Denmark, Shugol's U.S. team helped convince the International Committee on Sports for the Disabled that riding was a viable competitive sport for disabled individuals. At the resulting equestrian competition in the 1984 International Games for the Disabled, Wendy took silver and gold medals in dressage events. In 1988 she began riding competitively for the first time in nondisabled dressage events— and has placed well.

Shugol, who when not on a horse or in the water uses a wheelchair and crutches to get around, was introduced to serious horseback riding when she went on a 150-mile horsepacking trip in Montana. In 1979, when the first competition for disabled riders was held in New Haven, Connecticut, Shugol was there. She was partnered with a Morgan mare named Whippoorwill Hello, who later became her permanent mount and trusted friend.

Shugol explains her love of horseback riding this way:

"For one thing, it gives me a tremendous lift, because it is nearly the only sport I can participate in where I am absolutely free. I have four good legs under me, and I can keep up with any able-bodied person who happens to be riding with me. On the ground, I'm always lagging behind and asking people to wait up for me. But on a horse, I can go just as fast as any able-bodied person or even pull ahead of them. I might even be a better rider than they are or be able to go faster than they can."

equilibrium, most amputees who ride prefer to wear prosthetic limbs because they make riding more graceful and natural.

Some wheelchair users mount the horse from an approach ramp constructed of concrete or wood. For the person who walks but has difficulty mounting a horse, a mounting platform of two or three steps might be helpful.

A safety helmet is a standard safety precaution for all riders.

Riding Programs

Most riding programs available today are therapeutic in nature, and most people with disabilities that cause balance difficulties begin riding in therapeutic programs. Although the United States has been less ambitious than some other nations in promoting riding among people with disabilities, excellent American centers have been created through the North American Riding for the Handicapped Association (NARHA) and other organizations.

First established in 1968, NARHA is affiliated with some 426 riding centers throughout the United States and Canada. Each year NARHA serves about 15,000 disabled persons with the aid of nearly 25,000 volunteers who teach and assist with the programs. There is usually no charge to students. All of NARHA's affiliated programs must be insured, fulfill tough standards, practice stringent safety precautions and give their volunteer instructors rigorous training.

The NARHA program stresses safety first. All trainees must have a

physician's permission to participate, and the program staff must have a full medical description of the trainee's disability.

Safety equipment is available at most NARHA centers for use by people with disabilities. Most trainees begin riding with trained assistants (side walkers) walking on each side of the horse and a third walker who leads it. Belts with handles are attached to the rider on each side. The belts are held by side walkers until the rider develops sufficient balance and rhythm to ride unaided. A safety helmet is always required, and safety stirrups are often used, depending on the rider's disability.

Of course, a well-trained and cooperative horse makes learning to ride a

◀ *James Brady, former White House Press Secretary, enjoys a trip to the Therapeutic Riding Center, in Washington, D.C., with former First Lady Nancy Reagan.*

great deal easier. According to Dr. Wolfgang Heripetz, a German pioneer in therapeutic riding, the horse, mankind's helpmate and sports companion for centuries, has been given a special task—to be a partner in the treatment and rehabilitation of the disabled. However, just some horses qualify—it would be very difficult to develop equestrian skills or to have fun while fighting a temperamental horse or one with an uneven gait.

Anyone who rides for pleasure, therapy or sport understands that good riding results from mutual confidence and effort on the part of the rider, the horse and the instructor or coach. It means being taught the correct thing to do and doing it over and over again until muscles accom-

PROFILE

James Brady

James Brady, White House Press Secretary during the Reagan administration, is partially paralyzed from a head injury incurred when would-be assassin John Hinckley, Jr., shot and wounded both Brady and the President in 1981. Since then, Brady has engaged in a seven-year marathon of physical, occupational and speech therapy in which his fierce tenacity and ever-ready humor have served him well. He says, "You must be persistent and maintain a sense of humor. If I didn't have a sense of humor, I think they would have carted me off a long time ago."

In order to speed his recovery, Brady's therapists suggested he enroll in a therapeutic riding program in Washington, D.C. Brady loves animals and the outdoors, but he had a lot to learn: "At first, let me tell you, I was really intimidated by the horse, the trainers, and all the attention, but as time passed, I realized that riding is a matter of communication between horse and rider. I gradually relaxed and let my intuition take over, and I was able to direct the horse with more and more certainty. From a therapeutic standpoint, riding provided an advanced form of physical therapy that forced me to concentrate in ways I never knew possible. I wonder if John Wayne would have understood what I mean!"

modate and strengthen and reactions become automatic. The amount of learning time is a variable that all riders face, whether disabled or not, and is strongly influenced by both motivation and saddle time. Good riding instruction begins with teaching the rider how to maintain a secure seat on the horse. Once this is achieved, students are ready to develop skills for advanced performance and competition.

Competition

Currently graduates of therapeutic programs can find few riding opportunities in commercial stables and ranches, partly because instructors may have little experience or feel uncomfortable working with disabled riders. In such cases, disabled riders must sell themselves and their abilities to potential instructors and facilities.

The United States Cerebral Palsy Association offers events that follow NARHA guidelines and are based on those now in use in horse shows sanctioned by the American Horse Shows Association. Competitive classes are offered to accommodate the many people with disabilities who have little access to other equestrian activities. Competition is offered in four areas: equitation-on-the-flat at the walk or the walk/trot competitions, obstacle course, relay race and dressage, which requires a high degree of sensitivity and precision on the part of both rider and horse.

Although some NARHA centers offer riding competitions for disabled people, such opportunities are limited. To expand competitive riding, disabled riders need to request that local riding clubs offer walking and trotting competitions for adults. If the request is accompanied by an offer of assistance in making arrangements, regular riding programs may well be willing to offer such competitions, which should attract beginning able-bodied riders as well as disabled competitors.

"An early slogan of orienteering was 'Physical exercise sharpens the mind.' It means that participants in a difficult task such as orienteering must be mentally alert to solve the problems of finding their way. Disabled participants in orienteering have an added incentive to increase stamina and practice techniques in wheelchair handling while developing mental alertness. The interplay between the two can be fun and very beneficial."[12]

Arne Yngström
Swedish Orienteering
Teacher

Orienteering

When orienteering, men and women with different abilities come together to test their skills at finding their way around an unfamiliar landscape by using a map and a compass. Orienteering offers outdoor exercise, the intellectual challenge of completing the course with the highest number of points and good-natured comradeship with fellow orienteers.

Orienteering is an enormously popular sport in Sweden, and several of the nation's 900 clubs have tracks that are suitable for wheelchair use. Although orienteering is less popular in North America, the sport is gaining enthusiasts in Minnesota and some other areas of the United States.

The physical effort involved in following paths up hills and over rough terrain makes problem solving difficult, so fitness training and wheelchair technique are most important. Success has nothing to do with good luck, since maps are very precise and detailed—the orienteer's

ability to use the map to find specific locations in the terrain determines his or her success.

Orienteering involves several different activities. In *free orienteering*, the orienteers attempt to locate each of several checkpoints, which are distributed over a wide area with many footpaths, such as in a park.

In *point orienteering*, the orienteers move from point to point following a path, ski track or trail. In *track orienteering*, the task is to follow a track marked on a map. Successful orienteers stamp their card at each checkpoint to prove that a stop was made. To make it more complicated, stops at distractors, or checkpoints outside the track, cause orienteers to lose points. In *quiz orienteering*, each checkpoint is marked with a number and a question. For example, to answer question 12, the orienteer must first find checkpoint 12 and then answer a question, such as "What kind of tree grows at the bend in front of you?"

Recreational Travel

International travel stimulates personal growth and builds self-confidence while promoting international understanding. Today recreational travel is possible for people with mobility impairments because of amenities such as rental cars with hand controls, accessible train and air facilities and national and state parks with accessible trails and campgrounds. The options are many—travel can be on your own, with family and friends or as a group experience. You can make all arrangements yourself or use the services of a travel organization.

A wealth of information and services makes travel possible for the person with disabilities—access guides, books, magazines and information exchanges. Special travel agencies and organizations promote travel experiences for people with disabilities. Furthermore, experienced travelers are usually willing to share travel tips and information.

International work camps offer a unique opportunity for people with disabilities to serve others—like everyone else, people with disabilities have a great deal to offer. In work camps, volunteers work for two or three weeks on community service projects while learning about the customs and culture of another country. Volunteers pay for transportation but receive free room and board while on-site. Work camp volunteers have renovated a farmhouse in Finland, worked with children in Turkey and built an antiwar museum in Germany. Some projects provide help for participants who require some assistance with personal care.

Educational exchange programs provide yet another approach to international travel. A year studying abroad and living with another family while in high school or college is an option, as are summer study programs designed to improve language skills or to provide specialized study opportunities. Disabled students have even spent time teaching English in Japan as part of an exchange program. In three-week programs offered in China and Sweden, participants learn about the country and people and often invite their hosts to visit the United States. Recently a group of disabled and nondisabled persons spent a month in Costa Rica, living with local families and volunteering in different organizations. Although accommodations were rarely accessible, participants with disabilities coped, enjoying the opportunity to share their skills in a new setting.

Mobility International USA (MIUSA) is a non-profit organization dedicated to expanding international travel opportunities for persons with disabilities. MIUSA organizes trips, provides information and referral services and publishes several videos and publications, including a *Guide to International Educational Exchange, Community Service and Travel for Persons with Disabilities* and a quarterly travel newsletter. For information contact MIUSA, P.O. Box 3551, Eugene, OR 97403.

Portions of this chapter were taken from materials or comments provided by Bernt Eklundh, Greg Lais, Annika Larsen, Ulla Ståhlberg, Susan Sygall, Wendy Shugol and Arne Yngström.

REFERENCES

[1] Engström, G. and Augustsson, L. (eds.). *Kom Igen* (Malmö, Sweden: Liber Förlag, 1985), p. 27.

[2] Ibid. p. 45.

[3] Ibid. p. 24.

[4] Corbett, B. *Options: Spinal Cord Injury and the Future* (Denver: A. B. Hirschfeld Press, 1980), p. 75.

[5] Lais, G. "A Remote Journey," *Palaestra*, (Spring, 1987), p. 40.

[6] Wilderness Inquiry II. *Adventure Trip Brochure* (Wilderness Inquiry, 1313 Fifth St. S.E., Suite 327A, Minneapolis, MN, 55414).

[7] Maddox, S. (ed.). *Spinal Network: The Total Resource for the Wheelchair Community* (Spinal Network and Sam Maddox, P.O. Box 4162, Boulder, CO, 1987), p. 118.

[8] Ibid. p. 116.

[9] Pride, P. "Bicycling and Tricyling Training Techniques." In Jones, J. A. (ed.), *Training Guide to Cerebral Palsy Sports*, 2nd ed. (New York: National Association of Sports for Cerebral Palsy, 1984), p. 67.

[10] Allen, A. *Sports for the Handicapped* (New York: Walker and Company, 1981), pp. 71–72.

[11] Engström, op. cit. p. 174.

[12] Ibid. p. 132.

CHAPTER
4
AQUATICS

Introduction

Since man first walked upright, he has faced the challenge of moving across water—whether by propelling his body through the water or on a craft above the water. An early and major innovation, sailing, harnessed the wind's power, thereby greatly increasing the distances man could travel. In recent decades, motors have been added, making travel much more rapid and greatly expanding the recreational potential of water sports.

Water activities are universally enjoyed. Most everyone likes being near water, whether it involves building sand castles, diving deep into the sea to explore an ancient hulk, sailing or waterskiing across a lake or participating in a swimming competition. Today the range of recreational water sports for people with disabilities is almost unlimited.

Disabled people take to the water in several kinds of boats, including powerboats, sailboats, kayaks, canoes and inflatables. In fact, the first-ever all-disabled rowing regatta, held on the Schuylkill River in 1981, opened up yet another competitive activity to disabled Americans.

This chapter on aquatics begins with swimming. Besides being a popular recreational, fitness and competitive sport, swimming is a prerequisite to participating independently in most water sports. Other sections highlight the skills and enjoyment to be gained from sailing, scuba diving, rowing and waterskiing. Canoeing and kayaking are covered in the previous chapter on outdoor recreation.

Safety in aquatics is a major concern for able-bodied and disabled people alike. Everyone should approach water sport with a healthy respect for the aquatic environment, along with a healthy dose of common sense, a fit body, swimming skills and appropriately selected and used personal flotation devices. Given these precautions, opportunities for challenge, fun and fitness in and around water are practically unlimited!

"Water sport improves fitness, mobility and agility. People with visual impairments can sense the resistance and lifting capacity of water, which varies depending on how you move: how body, arms, legs and head are positioned and how much air is in the lungs. . . . Underwater diving gives a feeling of soaring in a state of weightlessness. . . . it's like experiencing a whole new world."[1]

Annika Larsen (Visually Impaired)
Swedish Sportswoman

Swimming

Swimming can be as simple as playing in the water or as complex as rigorous competitions. Swimming is a fitness and recreational sport that appeals to virtually everyone who pauses on a hot summer's day along the shores of lakes, bays and oceanfronts throughout the land. Many communities and high schools sponsor swimming programs, and many private homes and clubs have pools as recreational amenities. Furthermore, swimming is almost always recommended for participating independently in other water activities such as kayaking, canoeing, sailing and scuba diving.

Swimming is an untraceably ancient activity. Competitive swimming events were held by the ancient Greeks, although they were not included in the Olympics. The next written record of competitive swimming appears in 36 B.C. in Japan, during the reign of Emperor Sugiu. More recently, swimming has been an event in the modern Olympics since they began in 1896.

Swimming is an important competitive sport for people with disabilities. At the 1980 International Games for the Disabled in Arnheim, Holland, American swimmers brought home 38 medals. A dazzling performer was 16-year-old Triscia Zorn, who is legally blind. She won an impressive total of seven gold medals and set seven world records. She was judged to be far and away the outstanding athlete in the Games. Triscia regularly competes against sighted athletes and has been rated one of the best backstrokers in the United States.

"MS is a disease which makes you feel fatigued. Frequently I will say to myself, 'Oh, no, there is no way that I can drag myself over to the pool and teach those disabled children.' But the kids just pull me out of it. It isn't the children, however, it is the water. It is the best place for me to be."[2]

Kathy Plant *(Multiple Sclerosis)*
Swimming Coach

She was a member of the 1988 University of Nebraska varsity swim team.

Because water provides buoyancy, many people with physical disabilities feel better able to move—freer and less disabled—when in the water. The body is relatively weightless in water, and the feeling of being able to stand on weak legs or to move weak arms offers a strong motivation to participate in aquatic activities.

Historically, water activities have been used to lessen tensions and assist with rehabilitation programs. The famous Roman baths were originally constructed for use by battle-weary Roman soldiers. Swimming and water exercise were used routinely in rehabilitation programs for wounded soldiers during and after World War II, and water therapy continues to be an important part of many rehabilitation programs today.

Besides being fun, aquatics programs promote physical fitness and well-being for people of all ages and at all stages of physical fitness. Water exercise contributes to good muscle tone, flexibility, posture, breathing, coordination, endurance, range of motion, overall fitness and release of stress. What more could anyone want? An additional benefit is that

swimming does not traumatize sensitive body parts, and injuries are rare. Furthermore, water sports provide competitive fun, and success in water often leads to greater self-confidence on shore.

Swimming Strokes

The elementary backstroke is considered by many to be the best and easiest beginning swimming stroke, partly because the breathing passage is free and because some disabling conditions make other strokes difficult or impossible. On the other hand, when doing the backstroke, the beginning swimmer may feel that the body is tipping over and become somewhat disoriented. However, because a first step in learning to swim is learning to float, these problems are quickly overcome.

Four basic strokes are used in competitive swimming. The backstroke or back crawl is usually the easiest stroke for competitive swimmers with lower-leg amputations who swim without a prosthesis, as the swimmer can compensate to a large degree by using arms and upper-body strength.

The freestyle or front crawl is usually learned next and is the preferred stroke of many people. The breaststroke and butterfly are advanced strokes that may be difficult to teach and difficult for people with some disabilities to execute.

Persons with amputations or paraplegia may find that the body's center of balance has changed and may try to regain balance through small movements of hands, arms and legs.

Such movements are not usually necessary, however, and in the long run reduce swimming speed.

Training and Conditioning

Swimming is excellent fitness training that uses many different muscles without danger of trauma. A daily swim can be more stimulating, however, if simple goals are set, whether they are to stay active in the water a longer time each day or to swim a longer distance in less time.

Training for competitive events does not differ from training in ordinary swim clubs. In fact, many competitive swimmers with disabilities train with regular local swimming teams. As for able-bodied swimmers, training for disabled swimmers focuses on fitness training, technique and speed.

Technique training is particularly important because disabled swimmers must compensate for disabled body parts. Developing suppleness is also important, especially for swimmers who walk with crutches or use wheelchairs, since these aids often lead to stiff, muscular shoulders that can restrain swimming movements.

Swimmers with cerebral palsy need to concentrate especially on breath control and motor sequencing to strengthen and stretch body parts, increase range of motion and counteract exaggerated stretch reflexes associated with this condition. Competitive swimmers improve their strokes through drills that address specific problems.

Perhaps one of the most difficult challenges facing the coach of

hearing- or sight-impaired swimmers is that of helping them develop or correct stroke techniques. Resourceful coaches use practice drills while giving verbal instruction on how the swimmer should execute the stroke. For example, to help swimmers develop high elbows during the recovery phase of the freestyle, coaches tell them to recover the arm by drawing the thumb of the recovery hand up the side of the body to the armpit after completion of the stroke. In addition, coaches may physically guide swimmers through strokes or have swimmers feel the movement of the instructor while he or she is executing a stroke.

To avoid swimming into the side of the pool, some visually impaired swimmers count the number of strokes required to reach the end of the pool. After swimming the required number of strokes, the swimmer kicks with one leg and holds one hand out to protect the head. In competitive swimming, the coach may tap the swimmer on the head just before he or she completes each lap. The swimmer and coach must know and trust each other for this method to be safe.

Competition and Eligibility

People with similar disabling conditions compete against one another in formal competitions. Competitive swimmers in all categories usually supplement swimming training with

land training, including weight training, stretching, running and wheelchair sprints and distance runs.

Training has produced results thought impossible in some classes. For example, several years ago a Swedish swimmer did a flip turn (a circular turn at the end of each lap in which the swimmer circles over and pushes off the end of the pool with the feet) at an annual international competition for paraplegics at the Stoke Mandeville Games.

The Games officials considered this impossible, given his disability, and a protest was registered challenging his classification. The classification was upheld—the swimmer had practiced 30 to 40 flip turns after every training period 7 to 10 times a week for months. The following year, 50 percent of the competitors in that class did flip turns.

There are a number of national and international swimming competitions. For example, an International U.S. Swim Team that competed in the Second International Games for the Disabled in Paris, France, in 1987 brought honor and glory home to the United States in the shape of several gold, silver and bronze medals. The International Wheelchair Swim Competition, first held in 1987 at the University of Santa Clara, just south of San Francisco, hosted athletes from nine countries. The water must be wetter in California, because 48 U.S. records and 18 world records were set during the competition in

the backstroke, breaststroke, butterfly, distance freestyle, freestyle and
other categories, including relays.

Adaptive Techniques, Facilities and Equipment

Most swimming programs for
people with disabilities do not require
special equipment. In fact, hearing-
impaired swimmers compete regularly with nondisabled swimmers, as
do some visually impaired competitors. A pool that allows wheelchair
access to the water is a great help,
however, for those with physical
disabilities.

Although no adaptive equipment is
used in competitions, various adaptations can assist the disabled beginning swimmer. The amputee can
swim with a prosthetic limb designed
for use in the water or with swim
fins attached to prosthetic sockets.
People with quadriplegia who have
difficulty swimming horizontally can
attach a flotation aid around or between the legs so that the legs are
lifted to the surface. Because flotation
aids change the position of the body
in the water, they should not be used
extensively if competitive swimming
is planned.

Some modern pools have decks
at water level or ramps that allow
wheelchair access to the water. Others have hydraulic lifts that can raise
and lower a swimmer into a pool.
However, for safety reasons, every

swimmer should learn how to get out of the water without the assistance of a lift or wheelchair. This task is easier when the water level is even with the deck. They should also learn to transfer from their wheelchairs to the deck of the pool. Cushions should be provided to prevent bruising or scraping the buttocks on the deck.

For those who may never swim independently, swimming and playing vigorously in the water in inner tubes can be fun and beneficial. Games of inner-tube water polo can involve people with a range of disabilities.

Before instruction can be meaningful for the visually impaired swimmer, he or she must become familiar with the swimming area. The student must be able to form a mental image of the pool and its surroundings and be able to move safely from the locker area to the pool.

The instructor can assist by walking around the pool with the student and explaining such things as pool dimensions and depth along with locations of stairs, wall ladders, lifeguard stands and diving boards. Both permanent and temporary pieces of equipment should be pointed out. Visually impaired swimmers who are well informed about the swimming-pool environment are less likely to become confused, lose their sense of direction or bump their head on an overhanging obstacle.

PROFILE

Magdalena Tjernberg

Magdalena Tjernberg is one of the most popular all-around athletes in Sweden. In 1984 Tjernberg was selected Sportswoman of the Year and Athlete of the Year in Handicap Sport. Born blind, Tjernberg won her first swimming championship at the age of 12. Since then, she has set four Swedish swimming records.

Her skill is consistently outstanding. At the 1984 International Games for the Disabled in New York, she took five gold medals and two silver medals. She surpassed her own record at the 1986 World Championships in Sweden when she was awarded nine gold medals, and once again in 1987 when she took 11 gold medals at the European championship in Moskva. In her six years of competition, she has broken about 50 world records, making her one of the most successful athletes in the world.

Obviously Tjernberg takes swimming seriously: "Sport means everything to me. It has made me take persons seriously no matter what kind of handicap they have. Sport gives me courage and mental strength."

Rowing

The world's first all-disabled rowing regatta took place on the Schuylkill River in Philadelphia in 1981.[3] Nine disabled athletes participated—three paraplegics, two double-leg amputees, two post-polio individuals, one person with cerebral palsy and another with spina bifida. Racing consisted mostly of head-to-head individual racing or sculling in which individuals with similar disabilities were paired against one another. All athletes participated in the grand finale, a figure-eight race. The event firmly put to rest the misconception that sculling, or competitive rowing, is not suitable for people with severe physical disabilities.

A specially designed, fixed-seat catamaran rowboat, the HANDICAT, made the race a reality. It is a boat that is difficult to tip, an important consideration for persons who are high-level paraplegics or individuals with spastic cerebral palsy. A fixed-seat boat, the HANDICAT also en-abled individuals to row who do not have use of their legs.

Training for the regatta began in Temple University's two Olympic-size swimming pools, using the HANDICAT and personal flotation devices for safety. Both coaches and team members had a lot to learn. Some athletes were tied to their seats to prevent them from falling over; others used shortened oars for greater control.

As a result of that beginning, in which the United States Rowing Association (USRA) was actively involved, rowing regattas involving disabled people now take place every summer in more than 20 rowing clubs throughout the United States.

The United States sent its first national team of disabled rowers to an international competition in the disabled division of the Australian National Rowing Championships in April 1988. Disabled rowers demonstrated their prowess to the able-bodied U.S. rowing world for the first time in the Empire State Regatta in New York in June 1988. That demonstration convinced all who were involved that disabled rowers row with as much skill, passion and determination as the rest of the rowing world.

Although the fixed-seat catamaran continues to be the boat of choice for disabled rowers, it has some problems. The rower sits comparatively high above the water, making the rowing angle less than ideal. Rowers who study the biomechanics of racing strokes continue to tinker with the placement of oarlocks and the best stroking techniques.

In 1987 a monohull shell outfitted with outrigger pontoons made its debut, captivating disabled rowers with its potential. Its trials proved it to be stable enough for operation by individuals with balance difficulties and no more difficult than the catamaran to enter and exit. Best of all, the scull looks and behaves much like sculls used by regular rowing clubs. This is important because disabled rowing is an activity associated with established rowing clubs, and having comparable equipment helps to promote a feeling of integration.

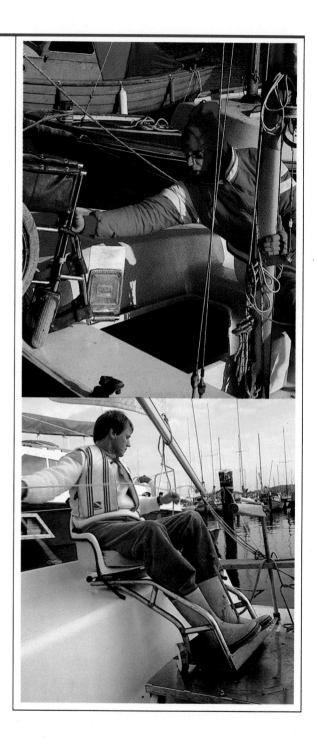

Sailing

Sailing is one of the world's oldest means of transportation. The America's Cup, established in 1851, is the yachtsman's greatest trophy and the oldest prize in international sport. Although sailing is primarily a recreational sport, it is also fundamentally competitive—whether racing or not, all sailors compare their boats, speed and tack with those of every other sailor in the water. Furthermore, sailors with similar boats organize competitions on almost any body of water large enough to support a fleet of sailboats.

Sailing can be a prohibitively expensive sport, depending on the size and make of the boat. In return for the outlay, the dedicated sailor gets cold, wet, hungry and either becalmed or tossed wildly about at sea. And when there is nothing else to do, the boat always needs cleaning and fixing up!

But sailing is a passion for many. For starters, the social aspect of sailing begins at the pier. The disabled sailor sits down while planning the route and says hello to neighbors who are sitting down in their boats. That gives a wonderful feeling of equality to someone who sits in a wheelchair all day. A pier of proper height that allows the sailor to moor the boat sideways makes the process of entering and leaving the mooring and boat easier. With some experience and ingenuity, most sailors manage to moor single-handedly.

A number of sailing programs cater to people with disabilities, including a full range of activities from model boat racing to sailing in specially designed keel boats to crewing on a training ship. A 171-foot British sailing ship, the *Lord Nelson*, accommodates disabled sailors who function as working crew while on board. Even international competition is available for disabled sailors—in 1987 the International Handicap Trophy in the Netherlands attracted 87 competitors in 29 boats from nine countries.

The Adapted Sailboat

The type of craft available determines the kind of sailing one will do. Therefore, renting or crewing on a boat before purchasing it is a good idea. Many novice sailors, both able-bodied and disabled, are initiated into the sport by participating in a sailing school that provides basic boat handling and safety instruction. This initial instruction gives the potential sailor a feel for the sport and its demands.

Physically disabled people use many different kinds of boats, from sailing boats with a centerboard to

PROFILE

Ted Kennedy, Jr.

Ted Kennedy, Jr., won a sack race at the age of 12, the first competitive sport event he entered after losing his right leg to bone cancer. Kennedy reported that it was no big deal: "After all, it is a one-legged event." Kennedy simply had more experience traveling on one leg than did the other competitors.

In the spring of 1974, Kennedy began skiing, working on his form and building up speed. He participated in the National Disabled Races and placed third in the downhill in 1982. Since then, he has been a member of the Disabled Ski Team. "Skiing," he says, "gives me the feeling of escaping from the limitations of being labeled disabled."

Kennedy has been active in sports throughout his life. He enjoys swimming, partly because water offers him greater mobility than movement on land. He skippers the family boat and has won the Edgartown, Massachusetts, Regatta as well as other sailing races.

To honor his ongoing commitment to an active life-style, the Boston Ski and Travel Show awarded him the Winter 1986 Outstanding Sportsman of the Year Award. Kennedy says a positive attitude helps people deal successfully with disabilities: "The right attitude is what it takes. You can consider something a big problem or a big challenge. The problems and obstacles you face are the ones you make for yourself. Once you alleviate obstacles, you can be successful. You just have to say to yourself, I can do that!' "

big family boats and catamarans. For example, a Swedish boat, the *Samba*, is especially adapted with a swivel seat to enable the sailor to remain seated while under sail. The variety of commercially available boats allows the sailor to choose an affordable craft that meets individual needs and is compatible with local boating activities.

The British-designed trimaran (a three-hulled craft), the *Challenger,* is an easily and safely handled boat designed with the needs of paraplegics in mind. A slide, hooked onto the main beam connecting the three hulls, eases transfer from wheelchair to cockpit. A customized seat, equipped with a cushion filled with polystyrene granules that contour to the sailor's body, is placed at the helm.

Little body movement is required to sail the *Challenger,* as tiller and mainsheet are within easy reach of the helmsman. The single sail comes fully battened, and a sail-tensioning device in front of the mast allows the whole rig to rotate so that the sailor can spill the wind from it.

The *Freedom Independence* is a 20-foot keelboat manufactured by a Warren, Rhode Island, boat builder, Tillotson-Pearson Inc. The boat is designed for stability and features an adapted cockpit with pivoting helmsman and passenger seats. All sail handling and trim functions can be handled from the cockpit. The boat is becoming popular—at the time of this writing, seven boats are in the water and five more are in production. In August 1988, a sailing regatta was held in Newport, Rhode Island, in which 30 disabled sailors enthusiastically sailed *Freedom Independence* crafts.

Sailing Programs, Organizations and Facilities

Sailing is increasingly possible for disabled boat lovers. For instance, in 1986 the National Ocean Access Project (NOAP) was founded to develop programs for disabled sailors. NOAP serves as a national clearinghouse for information on sailing and marine-oriented recreational activities for physically disabled people. The organization also works to improve accessibility to boats and marinas so that, for instance, a wheelchair user can maneuver onto a dock and gain direct access to a boat. Accessible restroom facilities in marinas are also a priority. In 1988 NOAP sponsored programs with instructional components in three cities, Newport, Boston, and San Francisco, and is planning to add several more in the near future. It also is a distributor for the *Freedom Independence,* sponsors a national sailing regatta and hopes to sponsor an international competition in 1989.

Washington State's Department of Services for the Blind teaches visually impaired persons to sail at the Sailways School of Sailing in Seattle. A similar program is offered in Boston at the Courageous Sailing Center. In Oakland, California, Glo Webel has offered learn-to-sail programs for disabled people since the late 1970s. The Water Sports for the Physically Disabled Program at the Mission Bay Aquatic Center, San Diego State University, offers sailing instruction on both catamarans and keelboats. The Sail Newport Sailing Center offers sailing instruction on the *Freedom Independence.* The NOAP can be contacted for more information about these and other sailing opportunities in your area.

PROFILE

John Lancaster

John Lancaster, an attorney and avid sailor, grew up sailing with his uncle in Hamburg, New York. When a Vietnam War injury left him paraplegic, Lancaster thought his sailing days were over until a Marine Corps buddy invited him on a voyage. That voyage convinced Lancaster that sailing was still feasible, so he purchased a sailboat and devised ways to make it accessible. Now he has spent about 20 years cruising in boats ranging from 23 to 45 feet.

Lancaster has participated in several major sailing events, including the 1987 Handicapped Trophy, an international race in the Netherlands. Later, Lancaster and his partner, Bill Murphy (also a paraplegic), won the 1988 Independence Cup, the first national sailing regatta for individuals with disabilities.

Perhaps Lancaster's most unusual race was the Ski to Sea Race in Bellingham, Washington, in which 289 teams composed of downhill skiers, runners, cyclists, canoeists and sailors raced 86 miles from the top of Mt. Baker to Benningham Bay. John Lancaster's team, the only one composed entirely of disabled athletes, completed the race in 60th place.

As executive director of the National Ocean Access Project, Lancaster passes his love for sailing on to others. The NOAP promotes sailing and other marine recreational activities for people with disabilities. And, he says, "Just have fun."

Göran Sjödén on Sailing

Water, water, water, at last, wonderful . . . a new world lies in front of me. No pavements, no steps, no traffic jams, no hills and uneven roads where I have to struggle with my wheelchair.

I look across the peaceful marina and prepare to board my *Samba,* an easy boat for the disabled sailor to master. I use the *Samba* chair to move from one side of the boat to the other, which is important when sailing a boat of this size. The *Samba* chair has a fiberglass seat fixed to a swinging stainless steel frame that is mounted on a platform that runs along the bottom of the boat.

I made control of the sails easier by equipping the *Samba* with a foresail that rolls up and down like a window blind when I want to reduce sail. I can now sit down in the boat and "pull the curtain."

How close to nature can you get? Well, it is hardly possible to get closer than when spending summer days in a sailing boat. The warm wind determines your speed and the cool water provides refreshing splashes. Rose-colored islands rise from dark blue water to contrast with the pale blue sky, and I hear the noise of sea gulls and a few fishing boats passing by.

We find a wonderful little island with a good natural harbor and grab the opportunity to swim. The boat is open at the stern for swimming, and I can move in and out of the water with relative ease. The open stern is also ideal for snorkeling.

I spend the night in a sleeping bag on the wide seats of the boat under a clear, starry sky and after breakfast start home. The wind is at the stern of the boat, so we put up the spinnaker, the thin, colorful balloon sail that catches the wind coming from our backs. It is a wonderful sensation to feel the wind catch the sail and push the boat forward.

Coming back home, the wind changes to a side wind, followed by another change that pushes dark clouds into mounds above our heads. We put down the spinnaker and climb into our raincoats. Soon the first drops of rain hit the boat, followed almost immediately by very heavy rain. The wind is still warm and pleasant, and I'm enjoying myself. What other activity would get me out into weather like this?

Back at the marina, I meet a lot of people who are more interested in my boat than my disability—a positive experience. This is a good way to reach people and to spread information about us. The marina has a pier that makes it easy for me to get myself and the wheelchair out of the boat and ashore. We tie the boat safely and set off for home in our car. Back home I discover, after a cooling shower, that my friend and I have achieved something positive and constructive, worth remembering. I warmly recommend sailing to everyone.[4]

Göran Sjödén (Wheelchair User)
Swedish Sailer, Sailing Instructor and
Boat Builder for Sailors with Disabilities

> "There are no disabled Americans—
> only Americans with varying degrees
> of ability."
>
> *Henry Viscardi* (Amputee)
> *Chairman, White House Conference on
> the Handicapped, 1977*

Scuba Diving

Maneuvering underwater is unlike any other experience. While in an almost weightless condition, the diver is free to move in any direction desired. Although voice communication below the surface is impossible without special equipment, the underwater world is filled with new and different sensations that are mysterious, exciting and add to the pleasure of the activity.

In 1970 a group of visually impaired Swedish scuba divers toured the United States with their instructor to demonstrate their diving prowess. Their demonstration proved the feasibility of scuba diving by blind individuals. Among other things, they demonstrated that blind divers are not as likely as sighted divers to panic in dark or murky waters and are not as subject to a feeling of being closed in or trapped while underwater. During one diving expedition in the Black Sea, the divers recovered lost articles from a sunken ship, including wine bottles 200 years old—an exciting experience for any diver.

Scuba diving is a sport of personal challenge. Since water is a foreign medium for all people, differences among individual capabilities are minimized and dry-land mobility problems are greatly reduced. The diver enjoys the sensation of near-weightlessness and can soar through deep underwater canyons and examine abundant marine life in an environment that plays no favorites.

The Handicapped Scuba Association practices what it calls *aquatic equality*, which means that during training, disabled and able-bodied students are paired. The program emphasizes abilities—the ocean doesn't care whether the diver is able-bodied or not, and every diver must be prepared to handle emergencies and take care of a buddy.

Accommodations for physically disabled divers are minimal, although substantial equipment is needed by all divers. Scuba divers must

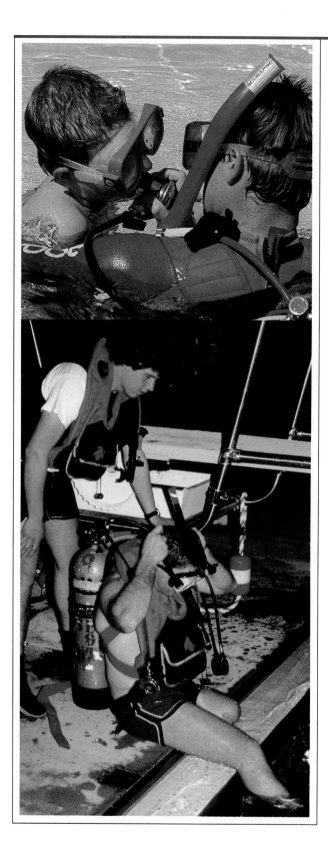

use costly and heavy equipment and carry it to the dive site, get hot and cold, wet, and salty and carry paraphernalia home, wash it and put it away in preparation for the next adventure. Thus dropout rates among scuba diving students without disability are as high as 80 percent.

Just as it takes a special able-bodied person to stay with scuba diving, it takes a special disabled person to put up with the rigors and demands of the sport. The diver must be comfortable in water, an accomplished swimmer and dedicated to the sport.

After completing a rigorous training program and becoming certified, for some a more difficult problem arises—getting oneself and a lot of cumbersome equipment into and out of the water. For disabled diving enthusiasts—and their number is growing—this is just part of the challenge!

Certification and Instruction

Divers must be certified as having the requisite knowledge and ability to operate diving equipment safely. For many years, national scuba certification agencies were reluctant to deal with disabled divers. In response to this problem, the Handicapped Scuba Association (HSA) was formed to address the needs of disabled divers and has been actively involved in both instruction and diver and instructor certification.

Considerable progress has been made over the last eight years toward making scuba diving accessible to people with disabilities. In particular, diver certification is no longer

discriminatory. Performance standards now consider the ultimate goal, not the means. Jim Gatacre, president of HSA, emphasizes that safety is not compromised in the standards. Although appropriate skills are always required, the actual method of performing a skill may vary from individual to individual.

When disabled people first began diving about ten years ago, diving agencies neither trained nor certified divers with disabilities. Today the picture has changed—most agencies certify disabled divers, and most of the discriminatory provisions in diving standards have been removed.

Now performance standards for certification consider the ultimate goal, not the means. For example, a diver must be able to enter and exit the water safely but the procedure may vary. The National Association of Underwater Instructors (NAUI), the Professional Association of Diving Instructors (PADI) and the YMCA all certify disabled divers and instructors. However, to date, no organization other than HSA trains either divers or instructors with disabilities. As a result, disabled persons who are interested in learning to dive must locate either (1) an instructor who has experience working with people with disabilities or (2) one who is willing to make the attempt and then learn through trial and error. Jill Robinson's book, *Scuba Diving with Disabilities,* provides practical advice for persons with kicking disabilities. Harry Cordellos' book, *Aquatic Recreation for the Blind,* includes a chapter on scuba diving for visually impaired divers.

Equipment

Divers come in different sizes and shapes, and their resourcefulness in adapting to daily life enhances their underwater maneuverability as well. According to Betsy Pillsbury, past president of Moray Wheels, a group of Boston-area able-bodied and disabled divers, very little in the way of special equipment is necessary for the disabled scuba diver, but extra care must be taken in equipment selection. Safety is the bottom line, and any safe solution is acceptable.

Those with little use of their legs depend on their arms for propulsion, for maintaining stability, balance, buoyancy and control, and for using lines, lights, cameras and spear guns. Divers whose legs do not provide adequate stability and balance use strategically-placed weights at the waist and elsewhere to adjust for buoyancy. Persons with limited manual dexterity who use buoyancy compensators will require a minimum of manipulation and sometimes minimal hand strength while still fulfilling their basic functions. Stabilizing jackets with soft-touch inflator mechanisms seem to be preferred.

People with lung involvement require masks and snorkels that are easy to clear. Low-volume masks and snorkels with purge valves are recommended equipment. Some divers use the gadget, a device attached to the front of the buoyancy compensator; others find the device too bothersome. The gadget holds the console slightly below and in front of the diver's face while the diver is in a horizontal swimming position. The

diver is thus relieved of the chore of having to stop swimming to check depth, air pressure or direction.

Diving for Visually Impaired Persons[5]

Although diving is considered a visual experience, persons with visual impairments derive great pleasure from tactile and auditory sensations underwater—the feel of current and water movements, the snapping and crackling sounds of tiny crustaceans, the sound of parrot fish munching on coral, the feel of hard and soft coral and sponges and the feeling of weightlessness.

Usually a sighted buddy provides underwater guidance and prevents contact with poisonous underwater life. A tether line connecting the blind diver and buddy serves as a means of communication.

Blind divers use hand signals, braille pressure gauges and a regulator that gives an auditory signal when air gets low in the tank as safety backups for air monitoring. Several methods are used to determine depth, including a line running from a surface float to the diver. Knots at 10-foot increments enable the diver to easily determine depths for making safety stops while rising to the surface; the diver simply adjusts buoyancy to slightly positive and ascends to each knot. Another method of depth determination uses a 60-cc syringe with notches marked on it to indicate 20-foot intervals. As water pressure increases with depth, the syringe moves down. The diver

PROFILE

Jill Robinson

Jill Robinson, a Washington, D.C., attorney who specializes in disability rights law, uses a wheelchair to get around when she's not in her favorite environment—underwater in scuba gear. Now an experienced diver, Robinson began diving after receiving instruction in 1982 in the YMCA's first scuba diving course for persons with disabilities. Since then, she has helped lead the effort to make scuba diving available to people with disabilities.

In addition to logging about 60 to 70 dives a season, Robinson assists with classes for disabled and nondisabled students. She is a NAUI and YMCA assistant instructor and holds certifications in night diving, deep diving, search and recovery diving, wreck diving, cavern diving, cave diving and Scuba Lifesaving and Accident Management (SLAM).

Robinson recommends that prospective disabled divers interview diving instructors until one is found who appreciates the opportunity and challenge of teaching diving to someone with different abilities—after all, teaching hundreds of people to dive can get boring after a time. However, she offers a word of caution: "Scuba diving can still be a difficult sport to break into. It was set up for nondisabled people. . . . you may have to be aggressive to break in."

Robinson has authored a book, *Scuba Diving with Disabilities*, which includes a chapter on attitudes about disability, "Disability Couth." She says that disability couth comes when people, both disabled and nondisabled, "rid themselves of stereotypical thinking." How to do it? "Hang out with disabled people who have had their consciousness raised, who have a sense of self-worth, who have become self-respecting and not accepting of patronizing behavior."

determines depth by feeling exposed notches on the syringe.

A useful communication device is a braille slate that lists the braille alphabet next to standard English letters. Sighted and visually impaired divers communicate by guiding the hands of the other over the appropriate letters. Alternatively, plastic cards with written and brailled phrases can be passed back and forth underwater. Plastic cards with written messages could also be used by hearing-impaired divers.

Diving for Hearing-Impaired Persons

Hearing-impaired persons who are fluent in American Sign Language—but not English—may have difficulty understanding the vocabulary used during training. New and unfamiliar terminology may be difficult to translate for these persons, so instructors need to be sure that all hearing-impaired students fully grasp new concepts before they take the written exam.

In cold underwater temperatures, signing is impossible if mitts or gloves are worn; techniques used by hearing divers (who of course cannot talk without special equipment while underwater) are used to communicate.

A note of caution to the water-sport enthusiast:
It is always a good idea to wear a personal flotation
device (or life vest) when participating in activities in
or near the water.

Waterskiing

Everything builds to that special moment when the towline tightens and the handle pulls hard against the fingers as a wall of water rises in front of the skier. This time, at last, instead of falling, skis cut through the surface of the water and the skier rises to skim triumphantly along the surface at approximately 20 miles per hour. This thrilling and memorable first time up is never forgotten, according to Harry Cordellos.[6]

Waterskiing is the most rapidly growing aquatic sport in the United States—water-skiers are found wherever a large enough body of water can be found, and disabled water-skiers are taking to the water in droves. Given adequate safety precautions, a powerful boat, good instruction and skiing devices already on the market, almost anyone who can swim can learn to water-ski.

"I've never let stereotypes—like a blind person can't do that—stand in my way."[7]

> **Bill Schmidt** (Visually Impaired)
> *Elementary School Teacher and Principal*

Safety Precautions

Anyone who skis must know how to swim and be water-safe, which entails being capable of handling oneself calmly in the water for at least five minutes. Waterskiing involves high-speed spills into the water. For this reason, a life jacket, or a personal flotation device (PFD) as they are called today, must be worn. A wet or dry suit may be desired if the water is cold.

Instruction

Cordellos suggests that blind students begin learning to ski in a swimming pool. As a first step, with the hands grasping a short tow handle, the student skier's feet brace against the overflow gutter of the swimming pool as the instructor pulls on the ski towrope. The instructor can point out important steps along the way, since the entire movement can be done in slow motion.

With this knowledge, the beginner then practices putting on skis in deep water, attempting to remain in a proper position while holding onto the rope. With the towrope handles in hand, the skier continues to maintain position as the instructor pulls him or her slowly through the water from one end of the pool to the other. A beginner who can keep the skis in a steady position in the pool should be able to duplicate the effort behind a boat with no difficulty. Similar instruction can take place on the beach or at a dock.

The trick bar or ski boom helps some disabled persons learn to ski quickly and efficiently. The boom consists of a bar roughly 12 feet long that is firmly attached to the boat and extends over one side (at a right angle to the keel). Heavy rope or cable is then attached to the end of the bar and hooked to the bow of the ski craft. The boom allows the novice skier to take hold of the bar and be towed through the water while maintaining balance with the hands. If it is strong enough, the bar can accommodate two skiers so that instructor and student can ski side by side.

PROFILE

Harry Cordellos

Harry Cordellos, a star athlete by any measure, did not begin sport activity until he was introduced to waterskiing at the age of 20. He was frightened. He had never engaged in any vigorous activity.

Born with glaucoma and a heart murmur, he had some sight as a child, but by the time he was 20, he was totally blind. He outgrew the heart murmur; the blindness remains.

Although learning to water-ski was initially frightening, he says it "changed my life forever." Now, in addition to waterskiing, he runs marathons and competes in United States Association for Blind Athletes swimming and track competitions. He has competed in the Iron Man Triathlon in Hawaii (swimming 2.4 miles, biking 112 miles and running 26.2 miles). He has run the Boston Marathon; his best time was 2 hours, 57 minutes, 42 seconds.

Cordellos is enthusiastic about sports: "All sports, but particularly running, have improved my confidence in my ability to do many things I used to think only sighted persons could do. Through trial and effort—lots of effort—I learned to overcome failure. You must never be afraid to try, and you must never be afraid of failing. To fail is not the worst thing in the world. After you have failed ten times, you will appreciate all the more the success that comes on the eleventh try."

Adaptive Equipment

A powerful boat makes learning to ski easier, as the quicker the skier begins to plane over the water, the less strain. A broad, square-backed ski gives the largest planing area and best stability for beginning skiers. A water-ski bra can help the beginning skier by holding the skis together. It can be made easily by attaching bungie cords to turnbuckles installed in the front and back of the skis.

A water board, or wave ski, which resembles a small surfboard but is designed for waterskiing, is available in sporting goods shops. It can be used for towing in a kneeling, sitting or prone position on the belly, or just for floating.

Various adaptations make water-skiing possible for just about anyone. The ski-seat, a floating pair of skis with built-in bucket seat, handlebars, foot bindings and foam flotation, provides a comfortable and secure position for the skier who cannot ski in a standing position. By shifting body weight from side to side, the skier can pivot the skis underneath and cut in and out of the wake. With additional modification, the ski-seat provides good support for quadriplegic and other disabled skiers with limited upper-body strength.

A new device called the mono-ski has a large surface area and metal apparatus that provide excellent stability. The pelvis is supported between bent supporting bars, and the thighs rest on a horizontal bar, making the skier secure but able to clear the ski easily in the event of a fall.

Portions of this chapter were taken from information, materials or comments provided by Anne Marie Ander, Louise Priest, Grace Reynolds, Jill Robinson, Göran Sjödén and Richard Towbin.

REFERENCES

[1] Engström, G. and Augustsson, L. (eds.). *Kom Igen* (Malmö, Sweden: Liber Förlag, 1985), p. 21.

[2] Allen, A. *Sports for the Handicapped.* (New York: Walker and Company, 1981), p. 36.

[3] Committee for the Disabled of the Pennyslvania Governor's Council on Physical Fitness and Sports, in conjunction with the U.S. Rowing Association. Adapted from *The Schuylkill All-Disabled Rowing Regatta* (Philadelphia, PA, 1982).

[4] Engström, op. cit. pp. 148–151.

[5] Cordellos, H. Derived from *Aquatic Recreation for the Blind* (LaBuy Printing, 1043 Folger, Berkeley, CA 94710, 1988).

[6] Ibid.

[7] Stein, J. (ed.). *Values of Physical Education, Recreation, and Sports for All* (Reston, VA: American Alliance for Health, Physical Education, Recreation, and Dance, Unit on Programs for the Handicapped), p. 4.

CHAPTER
5
TRACK and FIELD

Introduction

Track and field is an ancient sport employing basic movements traceable to primitive man. Athletics, as track and field is called today in international competition, includes many classic events that originated with the games of the ancient Greeks. From neighborhood playgrounds to the Olympic stadium, the challenge of the contest captures the imagination and fires the spirit of participants and spectators of all ages.

Track and field is primarily a competitive sport in which athletes attempt to better both their own personal records (PRs) and those of fellow competitors. Though it is always rewarding to be the best, it is not necessary to win Olympic gold to reap the benefits of this most challenging form of sport. For most athletes, setting PRs yields the strongest sense of accomplishment and personal satisfaction.

Athletes with disabilities have achieved extraordinary success in national and international competitions. In fact, many wheelchair racers who participate in major marathons throughout the United States and Europe achieve finishing times that place them among the nation's foremost amateur athletes.

Track-and-field events include marathons; short-, middle- and long-distance running; the pentathlon; throwing and jumping. Although each event has unique characteristics that require different techniques and sometimes technical aids, almost everyone can participate in at least one or more events. For example, people with little use of their arms and hands or who have difficulty with most activities requiring upper-

body strength can participate in wheelchair slalom using an electric wheelchair. Some individuals with cerebral palsy participate by propelling their wheelchairs backward or forward with their feet. Visually impaired athletes participate in most events with the assistance of callers who give verbal instructions or with sighted companion runners.

Improved techniques and intensive training for specific events have led to new world records in many disability classifications. For example, marathons have been won by wheelchair racers in less than 1 hour and 40 minutes, and the 4-lap mile was completed by a paraplegic wheelchair racer, George Murray, in less than 4 minutes in 1986. He clocked the exact time, 3.59:04, achieved by the able-bodied runner Roger Bannister of Great Britain in 1954 when he became the first person to break the 4-minute mile.

The many classes in competitive athletics are organized by national and international disability sports organizations. An athlete must be in good health and prepared to undergo intensive training and personal discipline if competitive excellence is the goal. To get started, contact a local disability sports organization. Remember, everyone can participate at some level.

Jumping Events

Jumping for height and distance has challenged man since early times. In fact, jumping skills were often essential to survival. The three classic track-and-field jumping events, high jump, triple jump, and long jump, challenge scores of disabled athletes each year.

A running approach is used for the three classic jumping events, although the purpose is somewhat different in each. In the high jump, the run-up produces maximum forward motion that is converted into vertical energy. In the triple jump and long jumps, the run-up establishes forward momentum and powers horizontal airborne distance. In general, no special or adaptive equipment is needed by disabled jumpers.

High Jump

The running high jump is a standard event in most track-and-field competitions. Fine neuromuscular control is necessary to execute the sequence of the approach, leg swing, takeoff, leg lift, layout over the bar and turn for landing. The discipline and coordination involved make it one of sport's truly artistic events. Acquiring such control requires extensive training, patience and attention to detail.

The technique used in the high jump depends upon the athlete and the disability. Athletes with physical and visual disabilities jump using the same basic techniques as able-bodied jumpers, with variations to compensate for difficulties with coordination, sight, balance and strength.

For example, Arnie Bolt of Canada, an amputee at the thigh, has won three gold medals in the high-jump and holds the world high-jump record for the disabled at 81.2 inches. Unlike most able-bodied jumpers, who *flop* over the bar and land on their back, Bolt does a dive straddle. As he goes over the bar, he rotates his body so that the trailing leg clears the bar as his upper body dives toward the ground.

Most amputees, however, essentially perform a front flip when competing in the high jump. The flip is awkward for able-bodied jumpers because rules require them to take off on one foot, while the approach for the flip is normally taken from both feet. Although amputees are allowed to use their prosthesis in the high jump, most abandon the extra weight and use a hopping approach on their good leg. Arnie Bolt's run-up consists of eight hops on one leg. Few who have seen his jumping would deny that it is one of the most beautiful and remarkable accomplishments in sport.

Cerebral palsied jumpers use essentially the same techniques as able-bodied jumpers.

Blind and visually impaired jumpers execute a shorter and more controlled run-up than sighted jumpers. Although mental imagery is used by all jumpers, it is especially important for high jumpers with visual impairments. For example, many visually impaired jumpers prepare for the jump by touching the high bar so that they can create a mental image of its placement and how high the body must go to pass above it.

Triple Jump

The triple jump consists of three stages. The individual begins with a run-up, takes off on one foot, lands on the same foot and takes off for the final action on the other foot—for example, left-left-right or right-right-left. The running approach provides

"As my faith had grown, my view of wheelchair sports had changed. I looked on the opportunity to compete as an opportunity for anyone who was disabled to rebuild confidence in himself, as well as rebuild his body. I was proud to be part of the effort and I had pride for everyone who participated. It didn't matter to me how well someone did as long as we tried. We applauded each other's efforts, receiving and giving strength to each other."[1]

Skip Wilkins (Spinal Cord Injury)

forward momentum, which must be maintained through the second action as the jumper makes a maximum effort for distance in the final leap.

This event requires perfect timing and the ability to control the body's center of gravity throughout the three phases of the jump. Efficient arm-leg coordination, the proper knee bend and the ability to divide the triple effort into its proper proportions are attributes of good form.

Amputees usually use their prosthesis for this event. Blind and visually impaired athletes use a short, controlled run-up and the assistance of a caller, who signals the direction of the run and approach to the take-off pad.

Long Jump

Although the running long jump is technically the simplest of the jumping events, it requires coordination, explosive force and fine timing. The challenge of the long jump is to gain as much distance as possible in a horizontal direction.

As with the triple jump, visually impaired jumpers use a relatively short and controlled run-up and take off from a runway that has a takeoff pad covered with chalk and a landing pit filled with sand. The length of the jump is determined by measuring the distance between the first footprint in the chalk and the point of landing. Amputees usually use their prostheses for this event, as they do in the triple jump. The prosthesis helps in building speed during the run-up.

PROFILE

Lars Löfström

Lars Löfström is an outstanding athlete who is recognized in Sweden as the first wheelchair user to be trained as a sport teacher. He uses his expertise, gained in wheelchair basketball, weight lifting and track, to analyze training methods for wheelchair athletes. In the 1980 Paralympics, Löfström was an important player on the Swedish basketball team, and he took first place in the 100-meter race as well.

Löfström began his sport career at a low point—after a traffic accident as a young man, he was unable to move about even in his wheelchair. Through hard training and participation in competitive sports, he realized his capabilities and eventually became an outstanding athlete.

Although Löfström played on the Swedish wheelchair basketball team that won a bronze medal in the 1984 Paralympics in Aylesbury, England, he decided that, to excel, he would have to choose between basketball and track. He chose track, and went on to win a silver medal at the World Championship competition in Rome.

Löfström continues to compete and has even perfected stunts such as racing down 120 steps in a wheelchair. He explains: "My purpose is to demonstrate that wheelchair sport can be as exciting as any other sport. I think that, by obtaining good results, I can help integrate sport for disabled athletes into the Olympics. I like challenge!"

The Seattle Foot

The Seattle Foot is a prosthetic device that gives amputees the flexible foot movement and push-off needed to run, jump and walk with a comparatively natural stride. It is one of many devices that have significantly improved the performance potential of amputee athletes in sporting events.

The prosthetic foot works by storing energy in a plastic inner keel when each step is completed, giving spring to the push-off for the next step or jump. The Seattle Foot weighs about a pound and is worn inside a shoe with a 3/4-inch heel. It must be fitted to the user, and it is available from orthopedic appliance specialists.

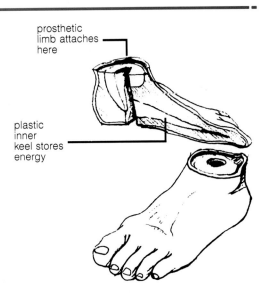

prosthetic limb attaches here

plastic inner keel stores energy

Marathons

Today disabled runners participate in long-distance races and marathons all over the world and are widely recognized for the excellence of their performance. Aspiring participants must work hard—they develop stamina by logging many miles each day in training and improve their technique through constant practice and experimentation. Many find weight training useful in increasing their strength. Of course, good coaching is always a great help.

The marathon represents the ultimate test of endurance and is the category of long-distance running best known to the general public. However, 3K, 5K and 10K races are the distances of choice for most runners, including those with disabilities.

Visually Impaired Long-Distance Runners

Visually impaired runners participate in long-distance road racing by

"You might think it would be boring to run a marathon or to ski great distances cross country when you can't see what is around you. But it's not boring at all. I love outdoor sports because they bring me close to the beauty of nature. I don't see the beauty, of course, but I experience it in other ways."[2]

Harry Cordellos
(Blind Athlete)

running with guides who describe the course orally. The guide and the competitor maintain communication throughout the race. They often use a short rope tether, string or belt to loosely tie forearms together, or maintain body contact by periodically touching arms during the race. The visually impaired runner also can use the sound of the companion's pounding feet as a guide for pacing.

Harry Cordellos, a blind athlete, has run in the Boston Marathon, the U.S. Marine Corps Marathon in Washington, D.C., and the Honolulu Marathon, among others, accompanied by sighted partners. Now in his late 40s, he has finished several marathons in less than 3 hours—a good time for any athlete.

At the start of a marathon, when runners are bunched up and it is easy to run into someone, Cordellos begins the run lightly holding his partner's hand or arm. When the pack has spread out and the danger of collision is reduced, he releases his partner's arm. They run with only

their forearms or elbows lightly touching, their legs pounding in unison. As they run, the sighted partner describes race conditions ahead and any obstacles that might impede Cordellos' stride.

Wheelchair Long-Distance Racers

Today many road races include wheelchair divisions. Times of wheelchair racers are reported separately from those of able-bodied runners. To date, the best wheelchair marathon

The Quad Backhand Method of Propulsion[3]

In 1985 Jan-Owe Mattsson, the world champion quadriplegic wheelchair athlete from Sweden, completed the Manitoba Marathon in less time—by 40 minutes—than any previous wheelchair athlete in his class.

Mattsson developed a new pushing technique, the backhand method, by accident. After Mattsson helped a fellow competitor who had suffered a wrist fracture make adjustments in a backhand pushing technique, the competitor, Stan Westermaker, soundly beat Mattsson. Mattsson promptly began experimenting with the backhand technique and soon significantly improved his own marathon time.

A number of marathon athletes who have learned the quad backhand method have greatly improved their performances and dropped hours from their previous times. Most racers use custom-designed racing wheelchairs that align the shoulders with the front of the hand rims. They add rubber or tape to the backs of their racing gloves to protect their hands and increase friction between hands and hand rims, which should be covered with rubber, tape or a treatment substance.

The pushing stroke begins with a straight wrist and hand contact with the rims between the 12 o'clock and 1 o'clock positions. As the hands approach the 2 o'clock position, the wrists are bent and hands rotate to the sides of the rims (Figure 1). By 3 o'clock and through the 7 o'clock position, the hands are on the inside of the rims, with the wrists bent. Contact with the rims varies from the ends of fingers and knuckles to the backs of the entire fingers and knuckles (Figures 2 and 3). At 7 o'clock, the hands flip from the rims and lift, beginning the recovery phase of the stroke (Figure 4).

The quad backhand method is one of many innovations developed in recent years to improve the performance of disabled athletes in track-and-field events.

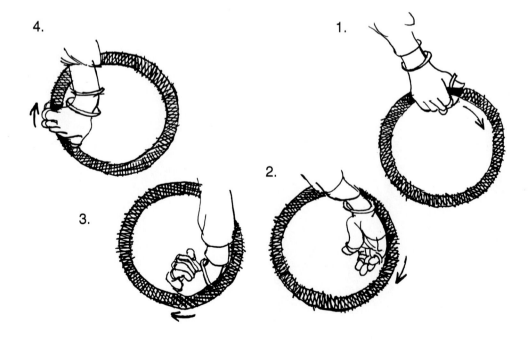

time is 1:40.14, set by Frenchman Mustapha Badid at the 1988 Seoul Paralympics. Of course, terrain and weather conditions greatly affect the times of both disabled and able-bodied runners and often play a major part in the final results.

In long-distance races, the wheelchair athlete's pushing capacity and form are very important—the racer aims for a lengthy forward push on the rims of his wheels while keeping rest periods between pushes as brief as possible. Wheelchair racers, like all runners, must have superb coordination, technique, determination, balance and stamina. Improvements in wheelchair design and racing technique have led to major improvements in marathon times.

In road races, wheelchair racers are usually started 5 or 10 minutes before foot runners, depending on terrain, to allow a safe start for all athletes. They run the same distance, and each group is timed from their own starting gun.

Running Events

Sprinting events require strong, well-developed musculature, quick reaction time, rhythmic coordination and an ability to relax at maximum sprinting effort. Long-distance running is a test of endurance, pacing and courage and requires a keen individual desire for self-improvement. Though physical attributes are extremely important, long-distance runners achieve greatness for reasons other than just physique, training and natural ability—they must have that elusive characteristic sometimes referred to as *heart*.

"Living your life in a wheelchair is what you make it, it doesn't have to be that bad. You use the chair as a tool to your advantage rather than a disadvantage."[4]

*George Murray (Paraplegic)
Wheelchair Distance Racer*

Today successful long-distance runners and other athletes who excel in sports requiring endurance are characterized by a specific muscle type, sometimes described as *slow twitch*, which is more rhythmic and slower than that of champion athletes who excel in events that require great bursts of power and speed. They have a muscle type referred to as *fast twitch*. For this reason, and because training routines are now highly specialized and designed for achieving excellence in single events, athletes rarely excel at both short- and long-distance running events.

In international running competitions, athletes are divided into groups and classes according to type and severity of disability. For example, among amputees, only double amputees with one or both legs amputated above the knee may use wheelchairs in international competition. (Wheelchair racing is discussed in more detail later.)

Due to the large number of classes, competitive events have many races. For example, the amputee group has five classes for the 1,000- to 5,000-meter races, and the cerebral palsy group has four classes in 100- to

PROFILE

Sacajuwea Hunter

Sacajuwea Hunter is one of the world's foremost wheelchair racers. At the age of 14, she was the youngest American to compete in the wheelchair track exhibition event at the 1984 Los Angeles Olympic Games, and at the age of 18, she was the youngest competitor in the 1,500-, 5,000-, 10,000-meter and marathon races in the 1988 games in Seoul, South Korea. Currently, she is ranked fourth in the United States.

Sacajuwea, a double-leg amputee since an accident as a toddler, began racing at the age of eight under the coaching of Bill Greene of the New Life sports program in Washington, D.C. She has been a steady medal winner ever since—in 1986, the Women's Sports Foundation of San Francisco awarded her its Up & Coming Athlete Award as a wheelchair racer in the Physically Challenged category.

Coach Greene, who affectionately refers to her as "Thunder," describes her ability: "She is relentless and steady. She comes at you all the time. The longer she pushes the stronger she becomes. She's in excellent condition and she's highly motivated."

800-meter races. There is also a 100-meter run on crutches. The visually impaired group has three classes. In all classes, men and women compete in separate competitions. Also, there are several classes for cross-country running events.

As in other events, minor adaptations are made in running events to

fit the disability. For example, blind and visually disabled athletes run sprinting events in the middle lane on ordinary tracks. Blind sprinters learn to run in straight lines, and with practice they become confident and relaxed, which in turn improves technique and speed.

For short distances, up to 100 meters, sprinters run one at a time, guided by callers or by sounding devices. Sometimes guide runners run alongside or just behind the visually disabled runner, calling out directions.

Wheelchair Racing

Wheelchair racing was introduced in the United States in 1956 by Benjamin Lipton, who organized the first national wheelchair games at Adelphi College in New York. Until 1969 the only official races were for distances of 40, 60 and 100 yards. The first officially sanctioned 1,500-meter wheelchair race was held in 1975 at the Pan American Wheelchair Games in Mexico City.

In 1971 the National Wheelchair Athletic Association's record for the 880-yard race was 3:49:06 minutes (3.8 yards per second). By 1983 the American record for 800 meters was lowered to 2:11:07 (6.7 yards per second). The frequent surpassing of records reflects the improvement in training, wheelchair design and the growing popularity of the sport. Like that in able-bodied foot races, the competition in wheelchair racing has become very keen.

In 1984, women's 800-meter and men's 1,500-meter wheelchair races were included as exhibition events in the Summer Olympic Games for the first time. This was an important step in society's recognition of the athletic abilities of disabled athletes. Wheelchair competitors hope they will be allowed full participation in future Olympic events. At the 1988 National Wheelchair Games, a large contingent of wheelchair athletes qualified for the Paralympics held in Seoul. The games, held immediately after the 1988 Summer Olympics, included more than 3,000 disabled athletes from 62 countries, representing mobility-impaired, cerebral-palsied, visually impaired, amputee and Les Autres athletes. Les Autres, *the others*, is a French phrase designating those whose conditions render them ineligible for competitions sponsored by other groups.

Wheelchairs Special wheelchairs are used for racing competitions. They are very light (18 to 22 pounds)

PROFILE

George Murray

George Murray is a man of many firsts and is often referred to as the "fastest man on wheels." In 1979 Murray became the first wheelchair athlete to break the 5-minute mile. In 1983 he cracked the 60-second quarter-mile, coming in at 59.2 seconds. In 1981 Murray and Phil Carpenter became the first wheelers to cross the United States in a wheelchair, traveling 3,442 miles from Los Angeles, California, to the United Nations Building in New York City in 137 days.

Murray became a paraplegic as a teenager, but that hasn't slowed him down—he has spent more than 20 years in athletic competitions, and he has parlayed his sports interests into a career. He is a wheelchair sports consultant, in demand as a speaker and lecturer, and he designs, produces and markets racing wheelchairs in collaboration with Chris Peterson of the TOP END company.

In 1983 Murray became the first disabled athlete featured on a Wheaties "Breakfast of Champions" cereal box, a place of honor for some of America's most popular athletes. Murray commented: "This was a victory for my sport. It gives a message to disabled children that if they want to, they can be athletes. Rather than focus on what they can't do, these young kids should focus on the things they can do."

in comparison to chairs used in everyday activity, have larger rear wheels (27 inches in diameter) and have casters and adjustable seats that hold the body in position and provide balance. Large hand rims are gradually being replaced by rims about one foot in diameter, especially for long-distance racers. The size of the wheels, frame and push rims selected depends partly on racing terrain, distances and the athlete's physical characteristics.

Lightweight Sport Wheelchairs

At least 40 lightweight sport wheelchairs are on the market, some of which are designed for specific use in sports such as basketball, tennis and road and track racing. Many of these chairs are customized to fit the individual user.

Most amateurs select an all-round sport chair, which they modify for the particular sporting event. Tires and casters are changed, and adjustments are made depending on whether the user wants to play basketball, run a marathon or attempt a rugged trail push through the woods. Wheelchairs today are a far cry from what was available 10 years ago; wheelchair design is a revolution that has opened all kinds of doors for active wheelchair users.

At least some of the following basic equipment is available in sport chairs:

- Movable axles: Axles are normally moved to pull the center of gravity forward, shortening the wheelbase so that the chair pivots faster. Long-distance pushers

lengthen their wheelbase to get more distance out of each push.

- Cambered wheels: Wheels are farther apart at the ground than at the top to provide lateral stability and a built-in tendency to turn. On some chairs, adjustments can be made according to the demands of the sport.

- Various casters and tires: Small, hard polyurethane casters are used for basketball and other hard surfaces; larger pneumatics are used for fast outdoor rolling on all four wheels. Large knobby tires are used for rough outdoor trail pushing where great traction is required. There are even wide flat-surface wheels designed for moving on snow or sand.

- Adjustment capabilities include:
  —seat and back angle and height
  —quick-release wheels
  —small-diameter hand rims
  —swing-away footrests and armrests.

Sports 'n Spokes regularly publishes information about lightweight wheelchairs, including an annual survey and occasional reviews of individual sport chairs.

Technique Wheelchair competitions are structured similarly to able-bodied running events. As in running events, different athletes usually excel in short- and long-distance wheelchair racing. For example, in the 100-meter dash, the athlete should develop a rhythm based on a strong, hard push and a swift recovery. Longer races require a different rhythm, based on a forceful arm thrust and a slightly longer recovery phase.

For maximum efficiency, the racer should use the recently developed circular propulsion technique. A revolving circular motion is made with the hands, and the grip on the hand rims is loosened just enough to allow repositioning. The forward push is followed by a backward pull.

Any training program's effectiveness depends on the overall fitness of the individual, and wheelchair athletes are no exception. For example, in preparing for dashes as well as distance races, wheelchair racers use a variety of training regimens that may include interval training, in which they run a series of sprints separated by shorter and shorter rest periods. They also practice sprints on uphill and downhill terrain, since muscles and the nervous system respond differently when gravity pulls the chair (or runner) in downhill sprints.

A person expends more energy while running than walking, and a person on wheels expends even less energy than one who is walking— when the surface is level. The wheelchair athlete, however, relies completely on upper-body muscles, which are much less efficient than leg muscles. Given a terrain with approximately equal segments of rising and falling inclines, a wheelchair long-distance runner probably expends about the same net energy as the able-bodied runner.

Although going downhill requires less energy of wheelers than of runners, wheelers pay the price when they wheel themselves and the chairs up inclines using only upper-body strength. Only the strongest, best trained and most determined wheelers make it up Heartbreak Hill near the end of the Boston Marathon.

Pentathlon

As it is for able-bodied athletes, the pentathlon for wheelchair users is an endurance and skill test in which results from the different rounds of competition are added together. Each disability category has its own pentathlon combination, which requires good basic fitness and training in several sports. For example, the wheelchair pentathlon is a grueling, one-day event for men and women. It tests participants' skills in discus, javelin, shot put and a middle-distance dash. Points are awarded based on performances in each event. The athlete with the highest total points is the winner. With some disability groups, archery and swimming may be included as a pentathlon event.

PROFILE

Monica Säker-Wetterström

Monica Säker-Wetterström, the best women's track athlete in Sweden, was proclaimed Sweden's Disabled Athlete of the Year in 1984. She achieved this distinction after winning five gold medals in the 1984 Paralympics. In addition, she participated in the wheelchair track demonstration event at the 1984 Los Angeles Olympics, placing second.

Säker-Wetterström became active in sports after an accident left her paralyzed as a teenager. She tried swimming first, then moved to track and field, where she proved so successful that by 1982 she had established three new world records during the Swedish Championships.

In 1985 Säker-Wetterström briefly retired from sports to give birth to a son, Alexander. She returned to sports in 1988, qualified for the Paralympics, and once again reigns as the best women's track athlete in Sweden.

Throwing

The historical significance of throwing the discus or javelin and putting the shot is well known. The immortal posture of the discus thrower, glorified by artist and poet since the time of Homer, symbolizes athletic prowess and presents a classic prototype of throwing technique. A perfect javelin or discus throw is a spectacular and inspiring sight.

Throwing requires strength and refined technique that can only be developed through intensive training. Time, patience and practice are required to perfect the timing of the turn and the throw. The athlete with the temperament to persist in training often surpasses the less conscientious competitor who might have superior physical potential: Those who work hard, regardless of their physical qualifications, are often surprised and elated at the distances they are able to achieve.

Basic throwing techniques that were developed by the Greeks are

PROFILE

Bill Demby

"If it hadn't been for sports, I think I wouldn't be here," says Bill Demby, a double amputee and world-class athlete who holds three American records in his class in shot, discus and javelin.

Demby is also a skilled wheelchair basketball player. In fact, television viewers may recognize Demby from his appearance playing basketball in a DuPont commercial. He has appeared on several television talk shows and has become something of a celebrity and spokesman for disabled sports. Demby thrives on competition and challenge, whether he's participating in a shot-put event, javelin throwing, wheelchair basketball, distance road racing or skiing.

Demby, who loved sports as a young teenager, was drafted into the army at the age of 19. In Vietnam a B-40 rocket hit the door of the truck he was driving, leaving him a double-leg amputee. During rehabilitation at Walter Reed Army Medical Center, Demby was reintroduced to sports by Jim Withers, a founder of the National Handicapped Sports and Recreation Association. Withers urged Bill to learn to ski. As Demby says: "I had it in my head. I actually survived Vietnam, which a lot of guys didn't, and I knew I would live to be an old man; nothing could change that. I was invincible." He not only learned to ski, he became a certified ski instructor.

At an international competition in Canada, Demby observed how seriously other similarly disabled athletes went about their training and determined that he would do the same. "When you see wheelchair users compete in skiing or basketball, you're seeing a real high."

still used by most competitors today, including disabled athletes. Adaptations are minor. Wheelchair users need a stable sports wheelchair that is anchored in place by a mechanical device or by a person. No help, apart from verbal orientation about the throw and direction, is allowed for visually impaired competitors.

The club, which weighs 397 grams (13.9 ounces) and is similar in appearance to a bowling pin, is thrown by people with reduced hand function. In other classes, traditional equipment lighter than that used by able-bodied competitors is sometimes used.

In wheelchair field events for the discus, shot, javelin and club throw, wheelchairs must remain motionless within a throwing circle, the dimensions of which may vary according to the event. The competitor throws into a sector marked by two lines measuring 40 degrees from the center of the circle.

An American woman, Janet Rowley, put the shot 8 meters, 9 centimeters at the 1980 Summer Olympics for the Disabled in Holland, an Olympic record for the blind. In the 1980 North American Games for the Handicapped, Rowley set new world records for blind athletes in the shot put and discus.

"*Sighted people believe that disabled people go into athletics only for therapeutic reasons. They tend to regard a blind athlete's accomplishments as significant only because they are therapeutic in nature. That's just not true, and it has a tendency to put us down. We disabled athletes go in for athletics for exactly the same reasons as nondisabled people. We have fun in athletic competition. We like having an outlet for our competitive instincts.*"[6]

Janet Rowley (Visually Impaired)
Shot and Discus Athlete

Wheelchair Slalom

The slalom event is a race against time in which the athlete follows a clearly marked path through an obstacle course that measures from 70 to 100 yards in length. The course is marked by pairs of flags through which the athlete maneuvers by going between and around the flags, backward and forward. Failure to negotiate a curb or ramp results in disqualification, while touching a flag with the wheelchair adds one second to the finishing time. The athlete with the lowest time in a classification is the winner.

The slalom is excellent preparation for wheelchair racing and other sport and recreation activity. Balance, endurance, strength and coordination improve with slalom training. People who use electric wheelchairs can join the fun and greatly improve their ability to control their wheelchairs in narrow places and on slopes.

Portions of this chapter were taken from information or materials provided by Ray Clark, Göran Johnsson and Julian Stein.

REFERENCES

[1] Wilkins, S. and Dunn, J. *The Road Race* (Wheaton, IL: Tyndale House Publishers, Inc., 1981), p. 220.

[2] Allen, A. *Sports for the Handicapped* (New York: Walker and Company, 1981), p. 48.

[3] Theuerkaus, S. "Quads Move Into the Fast Lane," *Sports 'n Spokes,* 12:2 (1987), pp. 24–25.

[4] United States Olympic Foundation. *Images of Excellence* (Boulder, CO: Videotape prepared by United States Olympic Committee, Committee on Sports for the Disabled, February 8, 1988).

[5] Ibid.

[6] Allen, op. cit. pp. 53–54.

"Challenge yourself to go after your dreams. Don't compare yourself with anyone else or you will work to someone else's limits instead of your own. Focus your attention only on those things which you can control instead of wasting your energy on things that you cannot influence or change."

Marilyn Hamilton (Paraplegic)
Wheelchair Athlete

CHAPTER
6
WINTER SPORTS

Introduction

Alpine skiing—the rush of wind against the face, the tingle of cold air mixed with the warm glow of the sun, the exhilaration of *schussing* downhill on skis, the pleasure of making a perfect stop. Words just begin to express why downhill skiing is such a popular sport around the world and gaining popularity among people with disabilities.

A number of people with disabilities are world-class athletes on the slopes and on ice. In the third Winter World Championship for the Disabled held in Sälen, Sweden, in 1986, the U.S. Disabled Ski Team accomplished a major first in international competition: It swept more medals in a single day than any other able-bodied or disabled U.S. team in history, bringing home 59 medals.

Most winter sports enthusiasts are not world-class athletes, however. Skiing, ice skating and racing, tobogganing and sledding, dog sledding and snowmobiling cover the spectrum from purely recreational activi-

ties to full international competition. And, unlike many sports, winter sports almost always take place with family and friends in a facility open to the general public.

Winter sports offer good fun and exercise in the fresh air. Some gear is required—warm clothes, good boots and equipment such as skis and skates. Many people, able-bodied and disabled alike, spend lots of time *chaleting*—sitting around in comfortable clothes with friends, eating and drinking by an open fire. For that, no special equipment is needed.

Several ski facilities in the United States accommodate disabled persons. Since most snow slopes and skating facilities offer no special facilities, however, the disabled skier or skater needs to check in advance to be sure that restrooms, chair lifts and other facilities are accessible.

The following pages describe skiing, ice skating and racing activities. Winter sport options are varied, challenging and fun—check out the

facilities in your area, pull out your mittens and boots and enjoy the bracing challenge of winter sport activities.

"You stand high up on the mountain with a long, well-prepared slope in front of you. The heart beats faster than usual, and butterflies disturb the stomach.

A last look at the view, put the helmet down, and pull on the goggles. . . . Off you go, and now it is a question of combining balance and technique to reach the bottom of the slope in one piece.

You feel that you are challenging nature by trying to master the steep slopes. Like mountaineering in reverse."[1]

> *Björn Carlgren*
> *Journalist and Chairman of the Swedish Handicapped Sports Federation (SHIF) Alpine Committee*

PROFILE

Diana Golden

When she was 12 years old and told that she would lose her right leg above the knee to cancer, Diana Golden's first question was "Can I ski again?" She could and did—the elegant Golden skis on one leg, using ski poles rather than outriggers.

Golden dominates her class as a seven-time world champion and seeks out the challenge of racing in able-bodied events. After she took the gold in all events at the National Disabled Races in 1988, Golden was named Ski Racing's 1987–88 U.S. Alpine Skier of the Year, the first disabled athlete ever to win that honor. She also has been awarded two other firsts for disabled skiers—the Beck Award from the United States Ski Association, which goes to the skier with the best international results in either Alpine or Nordic events, and the United States Ski Association award for Outstanding Competitor of the Year.

Golden also is unique because she was the first American disabled athlete to be paid endorsement fees by skiing equipment manufacturers, an important accomplishment because the fees help sustain her year-round training costs—Golden trains intensively at Attitash Mountain in New Hampshire. This year, for the first time, she will travel with her coach and focus primarily on slalom events on the able-bodied circuit. She thinks that the slalom holds great potential, pointing out that it requires tremendous quickness, with one recovery after another.

The hardest moments are not going into the race, but coming out of it, according to Golden. "The honors I receive are real honors, and a beginning. I look at myself as a beginner. I'm in racing, and I'm a good racer. I ask myself, 'Where and how do I go from here? I want to reach for something, rather than just maintaining.' "

Alpine or Downhill Skiing

Alpine or downhill skiing is the most popular winter sport among people with disabilities in the United States. About 10,000 disabled people ski downhill for recreation or in competitions using adaptations that make skiing accessible to virtually everyone.

Alpine skiing offers a uniquely exhilarating experience to persons with mobility impairments. Gravity provides downhill momentum, allowing skiers to achieve great speed and freedom of movement. A successful day on the slopes contributes to a sense of well-being and accomplishment—and a good night's sleep. In addition, the skier's can-do attitude and zest for living usually carry over into work and other life activities.

Organized downhill skiing by people with disabilities has a relatively short history. In the late 1940s in Europe and the early 1950s in the United States, World War II veterans with amputations began to experiment with skiing. Subsequently, the Swiss introduced crutch skiing, which opened the door wider for amputees and other mobility-impaired athletes.

It was not until the 1960s, however, that disabled skiing took off in the United States. During the late 1960s and early 1970s, persons with one impaired leg began to ski using techniques developed by amputees. During this same period, persons with visual impairments took up the sport. Sit-skiing, introduced in the early 1980s, made skiing accessible to many more people with mobility impairments.

Skiing, besides offering good fun, great exercise and exciting competition, improves total fitness and overall mobility. Leg amputees use skiing

for mobility practice. Persons with cerebral palsy develop more relaxed movement patterns. People with visual impairments improve their balance and capacity to orient themselves in space. Balance and coordination are improved among all skiers, and the exercise of large muscle groups improves circulation.

Adaptive Equipment and Techniques

Adaptive equipment and techniques make it possible for even severely disabled persons to ski. There are five major adaptive skiing techniques:

- Three-track skiing
- Four-track skiing
- Blind skiing
- Sit-skiing
- Other adaptive techniques

A Downhill Skier of High Class

Down the slope in long, beautiful, serpentine patterns came a skier who looked like nothing any of us had ever seen before. He didn't have ordinary poles. Instead of the round disks on the ends of the poles, he had fastened short skis that looked like crutches. The skier had only one ski, which he handled magnificently. He was a young man, perhaps 25, a casualty of war with an amputated leg.

As he came roaring down the side of the mountain, we were dumbfounded with admiration. We didn't stop talking about this Bavarian soldier who, in spite of a disability, had the imagination and perseverance to come back and recover his life in Alpine sports.[2]

Sven Plex Peterson
Swedish TV Sports Commentator

Each of these techniques is described below.

Three-Track Skiing. Three-track skiing is a sport for those with one good leg and two good arms. Three-track skiers use adaptive equipment called outriggers, forearm crutches with ski tips attached to assist with balance. Three-track skiing derives its name from the three tracks made in the snow by the two outriggers and the single ski.

Above-the-knee amputees ski with or without prostheses. The advantage of using a prosthesis is that it provides added support and balance, but it can be cumbersome and increase the risk of injury.

Some three-trackers, especially racers, learn to ski with ski poles instead of outriggers. In fact, that is how people with one leg skied before the invention of outriggers. Although more difficult than three-track skiing,

one-track skiing with poles is an advanced technique that is possible for many.

Four-Track Skiing. Four-track skiing is done by people with a wide range of disabilities who have two legs and arms, natural or prosthetic, and are capable of standing independently or with the aid of outriggers. Two skis and two outriggers are used, creating the four tracks.

Often a lateral stability device known as a ski bra is used in four-track skiing. It helps keep skis parallel and allows the skier to use his or her strong side to control the weaker side.

Blind Skiing. Skiers with visual impairments learn the same skills as able-bodied skiers. The ski instructor, however, must be a particularly skilled communicator.

A blind person must learn to use skis properly and techniques for

PROFILE

Lars Lundström

Lars Lundström, a Swedish Alpine skiing champion, was introduced to skiing by Ola Rylander, Sweden's *Flying Kilometer.* Despite abnormally short arms caused by a birth defect, Lundström took two silver medals and two bronzes at the 1982 Swedish World Championships. He went on to compete in the Winter Games and in 1984 won his first gold medal. In 1986, his best year to date, Lundström took three golds and a silver medal at the World Championships in Sweden.

Lundström participated in and won the exhibition races at the 1984 Winter Games at Sarajevo. Flying down mountainsides at nearly 150 kilometers per hour isn't enough for Lars Lundström. His next challenge? "To make a parachute jump, just to prove those wrong who foredoomed me to an ineffective life."

relaxing and making coordinated movements. Before heading down the slope, any skier must practice basic skills—turning, slowing down and stopping. The blind skier also must learn to judge speed. One technique is to feel speed by lightly dragging a ski pole behind.

Blind downhill skiers always ski with companions or guides who follow behind to watch what's happening ahead. If skiing in front, the guide could easily confuse right and left when turning around to see what the blind skier is doing. Sometimes, however, skiers with visual disabilities prefer to follow a sound, such as a small bell attached to the lead skier—it can reduce the need for voice communication. With experimentation, a procedure can be developed that is comfortable for both skiers. In general, the guide should be somewhat more skilled than the blind skier.

"It's an absolute fact that every day, on that hill, miracles are being performed . . . so many people with disabilities have been told they are very limited in physical sports . . . they experience the movement of skiing and realize their feet have taken wings. They feel free of limitations they may have felt before."[3]

Hal O'Leary
Director
Winter Park Ski Program

The two skiers must learn to communicate efficiently with one another. Clear, brief commands should be used—they often must be shouted—such as *right, stop* and *turn left.* It can be difficult to hear when surface noise is created by ice on the snow or when the snow is particularly hard. For this reason, a small walkie-talkie with headphones can help reduce the effort required to communicate.

Occasional rest breaks should be planned, since considerable concentration is needed by both the blind skier and the guide. Also, both skiers must agree in advance about how to get on and off the ski lift and which way to go. On lifts, skiers sit together, so communication is no problem.

Sit-Skiing. The 1980s introduced the exciting sport of sit-skiing for persons who cannot ski standing. As a result, people with multiple sclerosis, muscular dystrophy, cerebral palsy, spina bifida and para- and quadriplegia have become sit-ski enthusiasts.

The sit-ski, constructed with a fiberglass shell and metal edges, can be used on ski lifts. It is steered by leaning the body and dragging a pole on the side toward which the skier wants to turn. During instruction, the instructor skis behind the sit-ski holding a length of nylon mesh cord. The cord is used to stop the skier and assist with turns when necessary. When sit-skiers become proficient, they ski untethered without the instructor and safety line.

The mono-ski is the most recent development in sit-skiing. A fiberglass shell is mounted on a single ski, and the skier uses outriggers to con-

trol the direction of movement. Geared toward users with good upper-body stability, the mono-ski provides the same exhilarating feeling and contact with snow as that enjoyed by stand-up skiers.

Sit-skiing requires a hill with a relatively steep slope, since it is difficult to turn the sit-ski unless there is sufficient speed and momentum. The sit-skier, particularly when learning in a tethered situation, should avoid crowded ski runs because the skier and tetherer take up a good deal of space. Sit-skiers should also be aware of decreased visibility because of their close proximity to the snow when seated. With common sense and good preparations, people with disability-related circulatory problems will avoid frostbite and hypothermia.

Other Adaptive Techniques. This is a catchall category. People with one good arm and two good legs can use one ski pole; a pole can also be used with an arm prosthesis. Below-the-knee amputees who choose to ski using artificial legs usually use a heel line to achieve a bent knee position. Waist straps and thigh lacers help provide lateral stability and a snug fit, and they reduce pistoning and rotation. A special ski leg can be made for the amputee who decides to pursue skiing seriously.

Conditioning and Training

Ask any skier—downhill skiing is tiring and exercises muscles rarely used in daily life. Therefore, skiers must exercise regularly to build up muscle strength, endurance and flexibility before hitting the slopes. Like any sport, skiing exercises some muscle groups more than others. Therefore, pre-skiing exercises and conditioning should be tailored to the demands of the slope. Recent amputees in particular would be wise to follow a supervised program of strengthening exercises. If just one sound leg is available, it should be in optimal shape before the skier tackles the slopes.

While skiing, beginners should plan to rest as often as necessary by sitting down in a safe place off the trail. A burning sensation in the leg is usually a symptom of muscle exhaustion.

Competition

Several Alpine skiing competitions are available in the United States. In addition, *Learn to Race* clinics and training camps are conducted by several local instructional programs. Those interested in competition can race in programs open to the public, such as the United States Ski Association (USSA) races. Racers can qualify for national competitions at 10 sanctioned regional championships.

Both the National Handicapped Sports and Recreation Association (NHSRA) and the United States Association of Blind Athletes (USABA) conduct annual national championships. Both organizations select athletes for the U.S. Disabled Ski Team, which competes in international competitions.

Skiing Programs and Organizations

Much of the credit for increased interest in skiing is due to work and leadership provided by NHSRA. Its national training efforts, supported by chapters around the country, have introduced many disabled people to the sport and supported the development of many champion athletes. Five full-time professional ski schools and about 25 volunteer programs offer ski instruction to persons with disabilities.

NHSRA has developed a clinic team that trains instructors in adaptive ski teaching and advises on program delivery. It also conducts instructor testing and certification programs that are approved and recognized by the Professional Ski Instructors of America.

Nordic or Cross-Country Skiing

Nordic or cross-country skiing is becoming popular among people with disabilities. However, since the sport requires more muscular effort than Alpine skiing, it is not an option for some severely disabled individuals.

Participants include amputees who ski with prostheses and some who ski on one leg. Those on one leg rely upon upper-body strength and use ski poles to push themselves along.

People with good walking ability who need some assistance can use the four-track Alpine technique for cross-country skiing. Some assistance such as pushing or pulling with a rope can be provided, and frequent rest breaks are always a safe practice.

Although there is a sit-ski for cross-country skiing, sit-skiers need excellent upper-body muscular strength and endurance to push themselves

over any appreciable distance. Again, assistance and rest stops help. A well-prepared and well-marked track helps all beginning cross-country skiers learn quickly.

Cross-country skiing is well suited for persons with visual impairments who ski with guides or follow preset tracks in the snow. Two sets of parallel tracks allow skier and guide to ski side by side while the guide provides information. They must get on well so that the blind skier feels confident. To develop good rhythm, blind skiers and guides can follow each other or ski side by side, holding sticks between them.

When a well-marked track is available, some blind skiers manage unassisted. If several circuits are made on a track, a sound device such as a small bell can note when the circuit is completed or warn about a difficult area of the track ahead.

Since cross-country skiing is just beginning to develop in the United States, there are few instructional programs for people with disabilities. Those interested in learning the sport should check with a local cross-country ski resort to see if a willing and qualified instructor is available.

The competition programs described in the previous section on Alpine skiing also are used for Nordic skiing. Although in international competition Nordic events are held separately from Alpine events, the U.S. Disabled Ski Team participates in both Alpine and Nordic competitions.

PROFILE

Laura Oftedahl

Blindness did not inhibit Laura Oftedahl when she had the opportunity to become a disc jockey for a local radio station, practice her skills in public relations or ski. Rather, she says her biggest challenge is using time efficiently, since the demands of a public relations career and keeping physically fit make for a tight schedule.

Currently Oftedahl is the U.S. National Champion in disabled cross-country skiing. She won the silver medal at the 1984 World Winter Games for the Disabled at Innsbruck, Austria. She is a member of the U.S. Disabled Ski Team and says that she is the only member who doesn't live where skiing is easily accessible year-round.

Laura participates in different sports to keep in shape and improve her skiing proficiency. A favorite activity is tandem bike riding—her partner is also her cross-country ski partner. Together they participate in tandem bike races in Mora, Minnesota, where they have competed in a 50-mile tandem bike race.

Oftedahl is involved in sports in other ways. She organizes cross-country skiing and other recreational activities for people who are blind or visually impaired, including aerobics classes, cross-country skiing outings and learn-to-ski and rock-climbing clinics. To honor her involvement in fitness for persons with visual impairments, she has been presented with the Healthy American Fitness Leader Award by the President's Council on Physical Fitness and Sport.

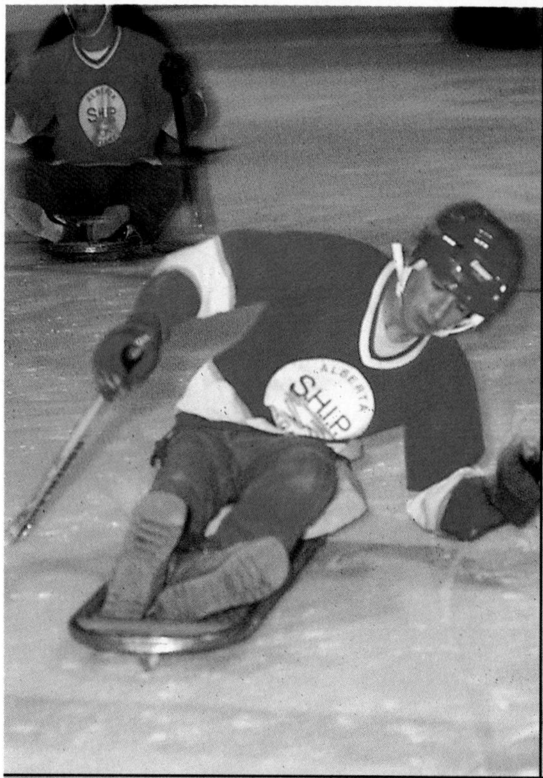
ALBERTA
SHIP

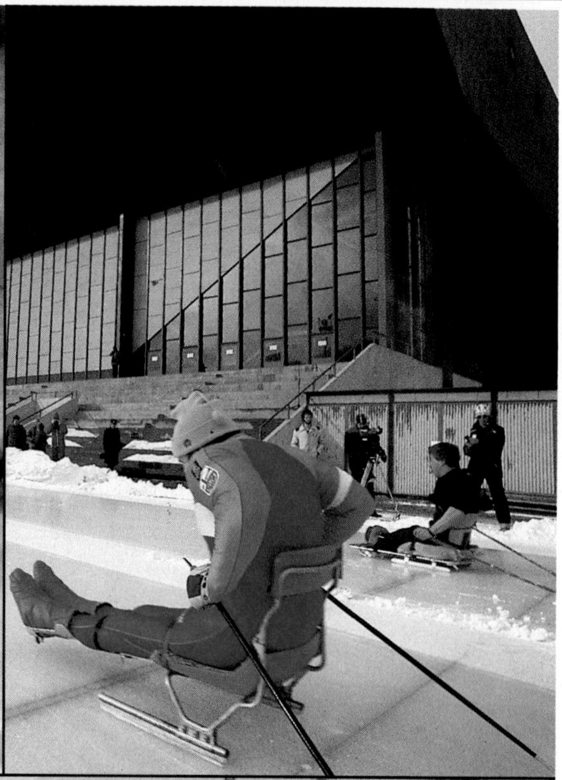

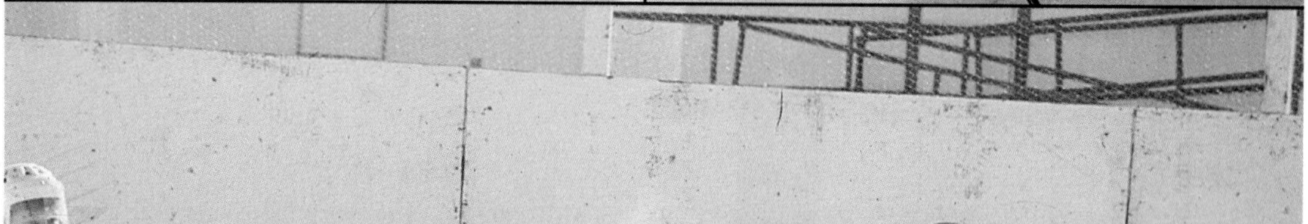
23
BLIZZARD
19

Ice Skating and Racing

Ice skating is a popular recreational pastime in colder climates. Techniques and adaptations used for skating are similar to those used for snow skiing. The outrigger skate aid, which consists of a figure-skating blade mounted on a crutch, increases the base of support and enhances balance. Propulsion comes from shifting body weight and a rotary motion of the arms, which forces the edges of the blade into the ice.

An adaptive device for the beginning skater is a skate aid, similar to a modified walker used by runners. The technique for using the skate aid is based on the principle of learning to skate while pushing a chair that provides support. The skate aid helps the skater maintain proper posture and balance and is more stable than a chair.

Ice racing, a new sport for people with disabilities, was introduced in Sweden when the first *ice sleigh* was developed in 1966.

The first international disabled ice racing event took place at the 1976 Winter Games in Örnsköldsvik. Another event was held in Geilo, Norway, in 1980. At the 1984 Games at Innsbruck, Austria, ice racing won official recognition. The 1988 Games for the Disabled included ice hockey and 100-, 500-, and 1,500-meter ice races.

Portions of this chapter were taken from materials or reviews provided by Björn Carlgren, Doug Pringle and Olle Sundin.

REFERENCES

[1] Engström, G. and Augustsson, L. (eds.). *Kom Igen* (Malmö, Sweden: Liber Förlag, 1985), p. 163.

[2] Ibid. p. 93.

[3] Maddox, S. (ed.). *Spinal Network: The Total Resource for the Wheelchair Community* (Spinal Network and Sam Maddox, P.O. Box 4162, Boulder, CO, 1987), p. 118.

CHAPTER
7
DANCE

Introduction

Dance is the graceful glide of a waltz in an ornate ballroom, the gyrations of teenagers keeping time to the sound of a heavy-metal band, the coordinated movements of a dance group celebrating their cultural heritage in a national folk festival and so much more. Bodies synchronized with music—more than any other activity, dance is an expression of our being, our beliefs and our feelings. Some say that it reveals the soul—the inner self.

Being able to enjoy dance is an important part of life. Dance is a popular recreational activity that is governed by our moods, desires and needs—a universal method of communication, an opportunity to express love, joy, social relationships, self-fulfillment and, yes, even aggression.

In prehistoric times, early man used dance to communicate with the powerful forces of nature—for a good hunt or a successful battle, to bring rain, to celebrate important life events or as a part of religious celebrations. Though the methods of expression were different depending upon the culture from which they evolved, each of the great civilizations embraced dance in one form or another. For most people in Western culture, dancing is primarily a popular social activity that requires only suitable music, a pleasant room and good company.

Dance has many variations. It can be performed individually, with a partner or as a group. Dance, as a performance, gives pleasure to audience and performer alike. Virtually all forms of dance have such common themes as joy, self-expression, communication and fun. The spirit and meaning of a national folk dance give insight into cultural history and pleasure and appreciation for its excitement and precision.

Dancing makes you feel alive! The fun of participating in a popular dance step or moving creatively to a favorite piece of music can easily be shared and enjoyed at some level by all, able-bodied and disabled alike.

Many participate in dance for its therapeutic benefits. In fact, there is a specialized field known as dance therapy that uses dance and movement in specific ways as a treatment modality. While it has valuable benefits and may be appropriate for some individuals, dance therapy is beyond the scope of this book. What is described in the following discussion should not be interpreted as dance therapy. Yet dance as a fun, social activity can be therapeutic in the general sense of the word for all people.

PROFILE

Sue Gill

Sue Gill's outstanding dancing abilities astound most people because she is severely hearing impaired. In fact, her instructors at the Stewart-Johnson Dance Academy in Trenton, New Jersey, often forgot that she couldn't hear their instructions. If she was facing away from the instructor, she wouldn't hear them until they tapped her shoulder to get her attention.

Today Gill is the assistant director of the Gallaudet Dance Company, nationally renowned for its innovative dance and signing routines. In addition, she is the director of the National Dance Academy of the Deaf in Washington, D.C., a dance-and-tumbling program for children ages 4 through 12. She also teaches aerobics and is the featured instructor on a nationally distributed exercise video called "Sing 'n' Sweat," which incorporates both sign language and voice into exercise routines.

According to Gill, the assumption on the part of able-bodied people that dance is beyond the reach of individuals with hearing impairments is something of a myth. She says, "You really don't have to hear to dance. You depend on internal rhythm. I use a drum. You can feel the drumbeat in your breastbone."

For Gill, dancing is almost a way of life. She expresses it best: "Dancing is a form of communication. It frees you to express yourself in a way that no other medium allows."

Dance is energizing! It provides opportunities for social interaction with peers and integration within the community. Dance improves flexibility and coordination. It also can improve muscle strength and cardiovascular endurance. It encourages a better sense of body image and confidence in movement. Social communication, body movement, physical fitness and self-expression are all important aspects of dance that can help each of us lead a fuller life. Persons with physical disabilities are no exception—everyone can participate at some level and reap the benefits of being involved.

"When I first came to Gallaudet [University] I was stiff and awkward, not very nice to look at. Dancing has made me flexible and graceful. I dance to enjoy myself, to get exercise and keep in shape. Schoolwork and exercise must be kept in balance; your body needs balance. Schoolwork, studying, means pressure, particularly at exam time, and when I come to the studio I can forget about it."[1]

Lily Chin (Hearing Impaired)
Dancer

Dancing Events and Facilities

Dancing events are arranged in a number of ways, including classes and social activities in schools, spontaneous dancing at parties, and classes and social dances arranged by local organizations. Dancing is best learned in small groups with the assistance of an instructor experienced in working with people with disabilities. Strengths and functional abilities of participants influence the form dancing will take.

Not all people are comfortable with all types of dance. It sometimes takes courage to expose yourself in this way. Some choose dance because it provides an opportunity for performing, while others, who may have difficulty expressing feelings or taking interpersonal risks, may need some encouragement and support. There is, however, some form of dance that is comfortable and suitable for everyone.

The primary accommodation for people with physical disabilities is to make adequate space available to allow for flexibility and wheelchair size. Adequate space for movement by a person using a prosthesis or crutches must also be considered. Individuals who have difficulties with mobility can and do adapt various traditional patterns of movement to capture and express rhythm.

An accessible room, a willing spirit and at least a hint of rhythm is all that is needed. Most of us would agree that music is also necessary. Yet dance can be performed without music, as is so beautifully demonstrated by the hearing-impaired dancers of Gallaudet University. Rhythm, however, is basic to dance. For some, rhythm seems to come naturally; others must work at it. Rhythm can be learned or improved by various techniques—clapping the hands, snapping the fingers, tapping the foot or moving the body rhythmically with the music.

The Gallaudet Dancers, a group of

hearing-impaired performers, are in demand in this country and around the world. Dr. Dianne Hottendorf, director of the group, differentiates between music and rhythm as she describes how her dancers coordinate their movements without hearing music:

"Rhythm is internal. Being able to hear the music has nothing to do with being able to dance. Although music and dance are inseparable in the minds of most hearing people, they are two separate arts. Dance does not depend on music. Dance is an independent art and can be performed alone. My dancers count the time, the same as musicians do. We work very hard at getting and keeping the tempo."[2]

Accommodations and Techniques

Some may think that a person without the use of limbs, eyesight or hearing is unable to enjoy dancing. Nothing could be further from the truth. Persons with all types of disabilities can and do join in the fun. Sometimes, as with other activities, the method of participation needs to be slightly modified to accommodate the functional strengths and abilities of the individual.

Specific techniques and movements depend upon the nature of a person's disability. For example, head or upper-body movements can be substituted for lower-body movement. Nodding can be substituted for clapping, wheelchair turns instead of twirls, one longer movement in place of two shorter ones. Dance timing may need to be altered according to the mobility skills of participants. Dancing is fun and provides good opportunities for socializing as well as for stimulating and regaining coordination.

Dancing for Hearing-Impaired People People with hearing impairments must rely on other senses in all aspects of daily living. Increased emphasis is placed on visual cues and touch as substitutes for sound. Since vision is a primary method of learning, the person assisting deaf and hearing-impaired participants must be clearly visible so that eye contact can be established and maintained. Images are very important in learning. Instructors should communicate with manual signing; they must speak slowly and clearly in short sentences to those unable to use sign language.

Touching is to be encouraged and should be used to guide the participant. Instruction can be clarified through hands-on movement of the body or by placing the body in proper alignment in relationship to other dancers, the surroundings and the musical accompaniment. Demonstrations by the instructor and pairing deaf dancers with partners who hear can also make moving to the music easier and reduce learning time.

A hearing-impaired dancer may gain a sense of beat and rhythm by increasing the volume of the music and touching speaker cabinets. Often dancers place their hands on the dance floor to feel the vibrations. Percussion instruments, amplified music and use of a hearing aid may help those with partial hearing. Also, instructors can convey the sense of rhythm through pronounced gestures and expressions.

Dancing for Visually Impaired People Specific oral instruction and touch are the primary methods of teaching movement to people with visual impairments. To be effective, directions should be clear, detailed and precise. Persons whose vision has been impaired for a long time, resulting in limited physical activity, may not have adequate experience to understand common terms used to describe movement, so words used to describe action must be thought out carefully.

Touching and hands-on physical positioning reinforce verbal instruction. Use of a patterning system can provide visual images for the visually impaired. With this method, the instructor demonstrates the movement that is desired, and the visually

---

"When I was small I was terribly shy. Dancing pulled me out."[3]

Sue Gill (Hearing Impaired)

---

impaired person touches the instructor, thus visualizing the pattern needed for the dance. Pairing the visually impaired dancer with a sighted partner is another way to demonstrate a movement or specific step.

Memorization of dance patterns is consistent with the type of learning people with visual impairments must develop for mobility and maintaining daily living skills—five steps to the door, turn right, and go ten steps more. The combination of this ability

and reliance on sound may explain why many have developed a strong sense for music and often excel at coordinating their movements with the rhythm.

Most instructional programs for blind and visually impaired persons provide classes in dance and movement in conjunction with mobility training. A person's body awareness and spatial discernment are greatly enhanced by repetitive choreography—regardless of the complexity of movements learned. The mastery of even the most simple dance routine contributes enormously to a visually impaired person's confidence and self-esteem—just as it does for all people. Carol Penn, director of the New Visions Dance Theatre in Washington, D.C., who works with visually impaired children, describes the impact of dance: "Dance is a discipline as well as an art form, and that discipline translates into your daily life. If you can get yourself together to be in a pair of clean leotards and tights, to be presentable in the dance class, and go through many monotonous and often very tiring exercises, then somehow, the way our minds work, that translates into 'I get up in the morning; I pull myself together; I meet my responsibilities and life goes on.'"[4]

Dance Variations

Dancing takes many forms—creative, ballroom, square, folk, ballet, modern and disco (or contemporary rock), as well as gymnastics and aerobics. As with all activities, more practice and training lead to greater expertise, providing unique benefits to all who participate. Many hours of practice and study are required for those who are part of a performing dance group and for those planning to enter competitions. But dance can also be enjoyed at very basic levels— moving with the rhythm, responding to the beat. Often simple rhythm instruments are incorporated into the dance—drums and tambourines— adding new dimensions to routines as higher skill levels are mastered.

Disco Dancing Disco dancing has declined in popularity among young people, but variations of disco are still evident in more recent adaptions. Rhythmical modern music encourages improvisation and creativity. Change is constant, but basic steps and movements often continue in new forms. Learning basic steps provides a foundation that can be applied as each new dance form evolves. The more demanding steps can be combined with simpler moves such as small taps or kicks. The wheelchair dancer can move forward, backward and turn around, as well as modify head, arm, shoulder and trunk movements to match the dancing partner's moves. This form of dance is particularly appealing because creativity of movement and innovation of style are encouraged and rewarded.

Ballroom Dancing Latin American dances such as the cha-cha, samba and rhumba and standard dances such as the foxtrot, Charleston, tango and waltz are very popular among people with disabilities. It is important to learn standard figures and steps with few modifications in order to participate as fully as possible in this most common form of dance. In Sweden and other European countries, ballroom dancing is an established area of competition. Fortunately, ballroom dance is becoming more common in the United States, though no national competitions currently are available for elite disabled dancers.

Folk Dancing Folk dancing, danced to traditional music from different countries, is a varied activity ranging from simple forms to those with intricate and quick moves and jumps. The easier dances can be learned quickly. They can be done without a partner and require only simple skills. Often they serve as effective icebreakers at social events.

American square dancing is a good choice for people with disabilities because it is based on a cadence of walking steps. Wheelchair square dancing has become popular, but it must be carefully planned to accommodate the size of wheelchairs. Sideways movements must be modified, as wheelchairs cannot move from side to side. Reducing the tempo by a quarter to a third helps wheelchair dancers keep up with the steps. Another method for equalizing different abilities is to add a singing verse to the dance. After the caller completes the dance call, everyone sings a verse of the song until all dancers have completed the call and returned home.

Wheelchair Dancing In recent years, wheelchair dancing has become a form of dance in its own right. The couple may consist of one person in a wheelchair and an able-

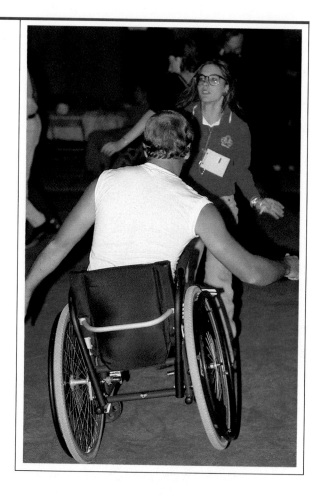

bodied partner. The movements of the wheelchair and the steps of the standing partner are carefully coordinated and adapted to each other to create a feeling of harmony. Sometimes the wheelchair dancer prefers to lead, particularly when dancing with an able-bodied dancer who lacks self-confidence or with a blind partner.

Many new forms of wheelchair dancing have been developed in Scandinavia, West Germany and the Netherlands during recent years. Although dance competitions have been held in these countries, it will probably be some time before international competitions in wheelchair

dance are established. Depending on the strength and functional ability of the individual, the main difficulty for the wheelchair dancer is coordinating chair movement with the rhythm. In particular, hand movements must be adapted to the music and rhythm transmitted in the form of rolling, stopping and turning. Each dance becomes a unique expression of the dancers' abilities.

Ann Riordan, assistant professor of modern dance at the University of Utah, expresses her view of the importance of wheelchair dancing: "You know, for lots of people in wheelchairs, particularly those who have little mobility, most of the human contact they have is with people who take care of them, feeding them, toileting them and putting them to bed, and generally that is not the caring kind of human contact that we all crave. Wheelchair dance gives them that; it's very personal. It conveys a feeling of intimacy. I have found dance is both an easy and a great way to communicate. When you dance together, it is easier to get a connection with people because it's communication without words. You can get outside the prison of your own skin and connect with another human being. We all have the same needs. We all have the same joys and feelings and thoughts. And we all think that's one of the hardest ideas to embrace, that we're all coming from the same place: we just have different colorings."[5]

Portions of this chapter were taken from information and materials provided by Jean Laine Kelley, Gertrude Krombholz, Sue Gill and Anne Riordan.

REFERENCES

[1] Allen, A. and Allen, G. *Opportunities and Programs in Arts for the Disabled: Everyone Can Win* (McLean, VA: EPM Publications Inc., 1988), p. 40.

[2] Ibid. p. 34.

[3] Ibid. p. 41.

[4] Ibid. pp. 50, 51.

[5] Ibid. pp. 60, 61.

CHAPTER
8
RECREATIONAL GAMES

Introduction

Many recreational games can be a source of fun and entertainment for severely disabled children and adolescents. As a matter of fact, some games described in this chapter appeal to both adults and young people who relish opportunities to compete and play active games in informal social settings. Often all that is needed to create a game is creativity, spontaneity and the desire to participate.

When devising games for groups of severely and multiply disabled children, everyone should be involved and allowed to experience success. Children should not be eliminated from a competitive activity unless an alternative activity is available or they can quickly reenter the game. Disabled children often have too much experience with failure and too little experience with fun and success in physical activities.

Most of the games described in this chapter are suitable for use with groups of able-bodied and disabled children, and integrated play should be encouraged. Children who play together quickly discover that similarities of interest and a sense of fun are more important than differences in ability.

Although group games usually are designed primarily for entertainment and fun, physical games serve other purposes as well. Severely disabled children often are isolated from other children much of the time and profit from the social experience of group

"Never check the actions of the child; follow him and watch to prevent any serious accidents, but do not even remove obstacles which he would learn to avoid by tumbling over them a few times. Do not too much regard bumps on the forehead, rough scratches or bloody noses, even these may have their good influences. At worst, they affect only the bark and not the system like the rust of inaction."[1]

Samuel Gridley Howe
Patriarch, field of education of the visually impaired

"Every child should have
mud pies,
grasshoppers, water-bugs,
tadpoles, frogs,
mud-turtles, elderberries,
wild strawberries,
acorns, chestnuts,
trees to climb,
brooks to wade,
water-lilies, woodchucks,
bats, bees, butterflies,
various animals to pet,
hay fields, pinecones,
rocks to roll, sand,
snakes,
huckleberries,
and hornets:
any child who has been
deprived of these
has been deprived of
the best part
of his education."

Luther Burbank
American Naturalist
and Educator

interaction, learning to share, taking turns and playing with others. Like those of all children, the muscles of severely disabled children need exercise and stretching, and physical games can help develop endurance, balance and coordination.

Let no one ridicule the leisure activities of another! What may seem very simple to one may be a source of challenge, release or satisfaction to another. A group engaged in a hilarious round of charades may appear ridiculous to another group that prefers to spend its energies trying to score a goal in goalball.

The first section in this chapter presents several minisports developed for use with severely disabled children and adolescents by Henning Svendsen, a champion Swedish handball player, sports teacher and author of a book on gymnastics for physically disabled students. A game called Bombardment has been added by an American contributor.

A second section describes Pickle Ball, a great *fun* leisure-time activity that is popular with all ages and ability levels. It serves many purposes—socializing with family and friends, skill development and friendly competition.

The third section describes parachute and circle games, which are immensely popular with children and adolescents. The final section describes several water games. Everyone loves the water, and severely disabled children are no exception. The games described just begin to list the possibilities. Use your imagination—everyone can play for fun and fitness!

Minisports

This section describes several mini-sports or games devised for use with severely disabled children and adolescents. Some are variations or adaptations of traditional games that are known and played by people around the world. The creative parent or recreation leader might want to use these games or invent others—imagination is the only limit. Often participants have ideas about how the games can be adapted and take great pleasure in being part of the creative process.

Games can be modified for pure whimsy or to accommodate a child with a special need. In games in which balls are directed at a target on the ground, a simple assistive device such as a plastic or cardboard tube about 3 or 4 feet in length can be used to assist children with severe mobility impairments. The tube is placed in front of the wheelchair and the child directs how it should be angled, raised or lowered so as to change the speed and direction of the ball. The steeper the placement of the tube, the faster the roll of the ball.

The child who has difficulty speaking can direct placement of the tube by using hand gestures or head movements. The ball is placed at the top of the tube and movement is initiated with a push of a hand, the head or even the tongue. The important point is that all players participate to the best of their abilities.

"Physical education can obviously contribute . . . to intellectual development by teaching what it means to compete, to strive, and to achieve. What's more, [it] . . . can provide a badly needed impetus to social and interpersonal development through group activities, and even stimulate moral development by teaching such things as fair play and team work."[2]

*Logan Wright
Director, Pediatric Psychology,
Children's Memorial Hospital
Oklahoma City, Oklahoma*

Land Ball

Overview: Points are made by rolling the ball into an area within sidelines and between a center line and the opponent's baseline.

Playing Area: Masking tape is used to mark the playing area, which is 10 meters by 6 meters and divided in the middle, parallel to the baselines. Teams sit across from one another behind baselines.

Materials: Colored balls or marked tennis balls and masking tape.

Procedure: Any number of players can participate. An equal number of tennis balls are distributed to each team; three balls per player is a good number to begin with. Balls should be marked or colored so that the balls of each team can be easily identified and counted.

Players stand or sit behind a baseline and roll balls onto the opponent's court across a middle dividing line. Balls that roll over sidelines are out of the game. Balls that cross the opponent's baseline become opponent's balls.

Scoring: When time is called, a point is scored for each ball that lands within the sidelines and between the center line and the opponent's baseline. If the ball is rolled too short and does not go over the center line, opponents win the point. If a ball is struck by another ball and rolls across the line, it counts as a point for the side on which it landed.

Variations: Plastic tubes can be used to direct the ball if a player has difficulty rolling the ball.

In a major variation, Million Ball, benches turned on their sides can be used to establish sidelines. A large number of balls, perhaps 30, is divided equally on each side of the center line and placed among players who sit on the floor. Tennis balls should be marked so they can be easily identified by each team. Each team tries to move as many balls as possible over the line to the opposing team's side. When time is called, the team with the most balls on the opposing team's side wins.

Million ball should be played in rounds. For instance, five rounds can be played and points added together. Length of the round and number of rounds played in each game depend on the ability and endurance of participants. Plastic clubs or bandy balls can be used to push the ball by players who cannot sit on the floor or who have difficulty rolling the balls.

Corner Ball

Overview: Points are made by rolling a ball so that it stops in a corner area marked off by colored tape.

Playing Area: Corner of a gym or room.

Materials: Tennis balls or other balls, colored tape, perhaps plastic tubes and plastic clubs.

Procedure: Individuals or teams roll balls into a corner triangle marked

with colored tape on the wall. Each participant stands or sits about 4 meters from the corner. The size of the corner and the player's distance from the corner can be varied according to the player's skill.

Scoring: A point is won if the ball stops in the corner; no points are awarded if the ball bounces out.

Variations: Plastic tubes can be used to direct the ball if a player has difficulty rolling the ball. Balls can be made of paper or masking tape.

Pocket Ball

Overview: Various objects such as small balls, tennis balls or beanbags are thrown into a pocket—a cone, hula hoop, box or tin.

Procedure: The game is played by one or two players. Distance from the pocket is varied depending upon players' abilities. Points are made by throwing the ball or beanbag into the pocket.

Colored-Ribbon Game

Overview: Two teams engage in hide, search and find activities.

Playing Area: Gym, recreation area or playground.

Materials: Two sets of colored ribbons about 12 inches in length. Teams are identified by the color of their ribbons.

Procedure: Numbers of players and ribbons vary. For example, each team of 5 players could be given about 15 ribbons, or 3 ribbons per player. Each team is given an area in which to hide the ribbons. For example, different pieces of gym equipment could be scattered around the gym at random, and this area would belong to Team A. Team B would have the changing rooms and corridors as its area. Each team is given about 5 minutes to hide its ribbons around its area. Then, the teams search for the opposing team's ribbons. The first team to find all of the other team's ribbons wins the game.

Bounce into the Vaulting Box

Overview: Balls are bounced into a vaulting box or other container placed about 4 feet above the ground.

Materials: Vaulting box and gym balls. When using the vaulting box, remove the two or three highest sections.

Procedure: Individual players or teams stand a fixed distance, perhaps 5 meters, from the vaulting box and try to bounce the balls into the vaulting box. The throwing distance to the vaulting box is marked off by tape.

Variations: The game can be varied by changing distances to the vaulting box. Teams can play if each team stands on opposing sides of the vaulting box. The ball can be thrown directly into the box or allowed to bounce two or three times before entering the box. Balls that bounce over the vaulting box are awarded to the opposing team.

Jerker's Game

Overview: Tennis balls are thrown (by teams or players) at an area of the playing field that is assigned high point value. Points are awarded based on the number of balls that land in the high-point area.

Playing Area: Two gym benches are placed about 1 meter apart and parallel on the gym floor, with seats facing inward. The playing field between benches is marked off with tape into areas of varying point values. For example, areas worth 2, 5 and 10 points can be marked off. An area worth extra points can be established 2 meters behind the playing area.

Materials: Two gym benches, tape and tennis balls.

Procedure: Each team (or player) is given 5 balls to throw from a point about 1 meter from the playing area. If teams are playing, each team should use different-colored balls. Balls are thrown, one at a time, with opposing teams or players taking turns and trying to place their own balls in high-point areas while knocking the opponents' balls into lower point areas. The number of balls used depends on team size.

Variations: Use different types of balls, such as soccer balls or gym balls, beanbags or balloons. Players

who have difficulty throwing can use a plastic tube to direct the ball.

Blind Alley

Overview: Players win points by getting as close as possible to a 10-point line while blindfolded.

Materials: Scarf and white tape.

Procedure: Blind Alley can be played by individuals or teams. Blindfolded players try to get as close as possible to a 10-point line; if the 10-point line is crossed, no points are scored. Lines of declining point value can be placed in front of the 10-point line. Other players must be quiet to prevent giving the contestant clues about his or her location with respect to the line. Someone should stand behind the 10-point line to be sure that nobody drives a wheelchair into a wall or other obstacle while blindfolded. A helper is allowed to push the chair if the contestant needs assistance, but the contestant must direct the moves made by the helper.

Sitting Handball

Overview: Sitting Handball is a variation of the European game of team handball. The game is similar to indoor soccer, except that players sit on the floor and throw the ball into the goal with their hands.

Playing Area: Players sit on a small court (about 25 × 50 feet); the size can be adjusted to conform to player abilities and room size. Masking tape can be used to mark the goal penalty area (about 3 feet in front of the goal) and the center-court line, which also serves as the free-throw line.

Materials: A suitably heavy ball such as a soccer ball or basketball and two goal nets, stretched to be about 2 feet high, 4 feet wide and 2 feet deep; masking tape for marking court lines.

Players: Two teams of 6 players each. Each team usually consists of one goalkeeper, two defenders, two wings, and one center.

Rules and Procedure: Players sit on the floor, placed in positions where they are most helpful in attack and defense. If players can move, they

must move to a new position after passing the ball to a team member. Moving rules should be appropriate to players' abilities.

Play begins when the ball is thrown into the center of the court. Each player may hold the ball for 5 seconds or less and bounce the ball along the longer sides of the court to pass the ball to other team members. The goalkeeper can bat the ball out of the goal but may catch the ball only when not in the goal penalty area.

Players may not move while holding the ball, nor pass balls to themselves by throwing the ball a short distance and moving up to it.

When a goal is scored, the ball is moved back to the center line.

Scoring: Matches usually consist of two halves of 10 minutes each. Players throw the ball to each other and make points by throwing it into the goal, which is defended by a goalkeeper.

Penalties: All body contact between players is forbidden, as is obstructing an opponent. A warning is given for the first offense; the player is sent off the court for the second offense. If the ball is held too long or a foul occurs in the penalty area, a penalty throw from the center line is awarded to the opposing team. The opposing team is awarded a penalty throw if a pass is made to the goalkeeper while he or she is in the goal area. During penalty throws, the goal is defended only by the goalie.

Wheelchair Bandy

Overview: Wheelchair Bandy is a game much like field hockey. Each team tries to score by placing the ball in the other's goal.

Playing Court: The playing court is about 20 meters by 10 meters; goals are about 3 meters wide and half a meter high. The penalty area in front of the goal is about 3 meters deep. The court should be surrounded by walls or gym benches turned on their sides so that the ball can be played off the sides of the court. The size of the playing court and goals can vary according to players' abilities, but the game is more fun if at least a couple of goals are made during the game—a no-goal game can easily occur if goal nets are too small.

Materials: Flexible plastic hockey sticks and a lightweight plastic ball. Players wear protective clothing—helmets, plastic glasses, seatbelts and straps as necessary.

Players: Two teams of five players.

Procedure: Although both teams may use clubs while in the penalty area, a goal scored when a team member is in the penalty area is disallowed. While in the penalty area, the goalkeeper is allowed to pick up the ball, hold it and throw it onto the playing court. When the goalkeeper throws the ball directly into the opponent's goal, it must touch another player first if the goal is to count.

Scoring: Playing time consists of two 15-minute halves. A point is scored each time a team places a ball in the other team's goal.

Rules and Penalties: Rules may be modified according to players' abilities, but sticking clubs into wheelchair wheels and other deliberate

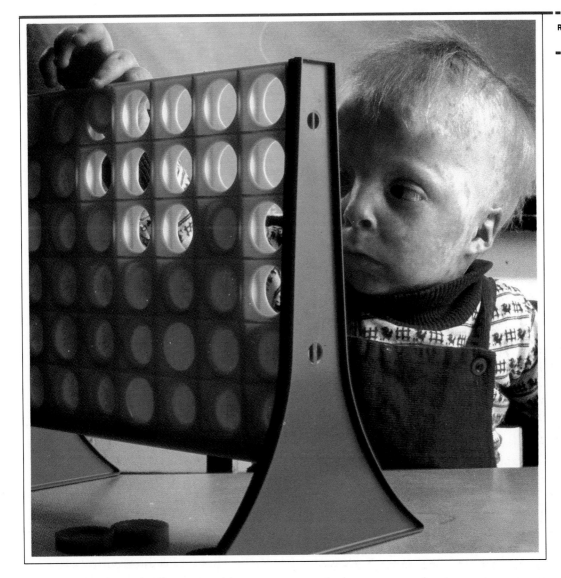

physical contact are always fouls. Players not using the proper playing equipment—helmets for all players, plastic glasses, seatbelts and straps as necessary—should be sent off the court.

The following actions are forbidden during the game:

- Touching the opponent or the opponent's chair with hands or club (a warning is given)

- Driving into an opponent (player is sent off the court for 2 minutes)
- Throwing the club on the floor, after the ball or at another player (player is sent off the court for 2 minutes)
- Lifting the club above shoulder height
- Touching and holding the ball in the hand or putting it in the wheelchair

• Passing the ball by hand to a team member

When a player is sent off the court, the ball is awarded to the opposing team. A penalty is awarded if penalty area rules are broken. When the ball is blocked against the wall, by the goalkeeper or touched by a hand, it is dropped between opponents, who scramble for it in a face-off. Substitutions can be made by getting the referee's attention when the requesting team member's goalkeeper has the ball.

Bombardment

Overview: Two teams of three to five players each attempt to drive a large ball across the opponent's goal line by hitting it with smaller thrown balls.

Playing Area: Play may be indoors or outdoors in any area where appropriate playing boundaries can be marked.

Materials: Large ball and a supply of volleyballs, soccer balls or gym balls.

Procedure: Divide the group into two teams with each taking position along its own goal line, and place the large ball in the middle of the playing area.

Divide the smaller balls equally between the two teams. Ideally, each player should have a ball at the beginning of the game. Each team throws balls at the large ball, attempting to drive it toward and over the opponent's goal line. Each team recovers balls already thrown and continues throwing until the large ball crosses one of the goals. Alternatively, a specified time can be called, and the team with the ball closest to the opponent's goal line wins.

Variations: Use more than one large ball or a large ball and other balls as targets. The distance between goal lines can be adjusted to conform to participants' abilities. Plastic balls or beach balls can be used as targets by players with poor throwing skills. Use goal lines that angle somewhat toward the goal, so individuals with poor throwing skills can play closer to the goal while those with better throwing skills are more distant.

Pickle Ball

Pickle Ball, a relatively new American game that is great fun, was developed as an adaptation of paddle ball. Wooden paddles are used to hit plastic whiffle balls back and forth across a low net. The game, which is popular with individuals of all ages and ability levels, got its name when Pickle, the originator's dog, dutifully retrieved the ball whether his help was wanted or not!

As with most physical activities, higher skill levels lead to faster games and greater benefits of fitness and good health. Even people with limited past success with physical games rapidly develop skill and achieve much personal satisfaction. The game is played with enthusiasm by many people with disabling conditions. Often no accommodations are necessary beyond some personalized instruction.

Commonsense accommodations are made for people with mobility impairments, such as permitting additional bounces before the ball must be returned, reducing the size or configuration of the court, revising serve requirements and modifying scoring. Through imagination, creativity and resourcefulness, the game can be adapted for people with similar or dissimilar disabilities and for play between able-bodied and disabled participants.

Playing Area: Pickle Ball usually is played on a regulation badminton court (44 feet by 20 feet), although larger or smaller courts can be used. The court is marked off with tape or painted lines on any flat hard floor or open area. The net is placed so that its top is 36 inches above the playing surface.

Materials: Wooden paddles, whiffle balls and badminton net and poles.

Players: Single or double play—two or four players—is possible. Some players successfully play *cutthroat*—three players organized as in racquetball so that one individual plays

against two opponents. Frequently, mixed doubles—male and female, able-bodied and disabled, children and seniors—are played.

Procedure: The game format is similar to that of badminton. Serves and first returns must bounce in the area between the net and the serve line before being returned. During play, when a player is between the serve line and the net, the ball cannot be played in the air; it must bounce before being returned. Between the serve and end lines, balls can be played either in the air or on the first bounce.

Scoring: Exactly the same as in badminton.

Parachute and Circle Rope Play

Parachute play was introduced in the late 1930s to a secondary school physical education class. Since then, parachutes have become popular and effective equipment for informal games involving students of all ages and abilities.

Children surround the parachute (or circle rope) and rhythmically walk, run, jump, hop or skip in a circle while bouncing the chute (or rope) up and down. Group skill involves moving in unison and holding the chute with uniform amounts of tension.

By skipping, running or moving in a circle while holding the chute (or circle rope), children learn to move rhythmically and in step with one another. They bounce a ball in the middle of the chute or bounce the chute up and all try to run under and out (while holding the chute) before it falls and catches them. Variations are many, limited only by the imaginations of the players and their leader.

Circle ropes are excellent for introducing parachute game activities and concepts. Obvious advantages of circle ropes over parachutes are that participants can see their feet and other participants at all times and movements are easier to perform successfully. As with parachute activities, individual imagination and creativity make circle rope play an appealing and extremely effective group physical activity.

Cooperative parachute and circle rope play is enormously popular with children of all ages because it is such great fun. At the same time, it develops physical and motor fitness, fundamental motor skills and movement patterns, and it can introduce rhythmic patterns from folk and cultural dances.

Parachute play is an excellent integrated play activity for children of mixed abilities. Visually impaired children can be paired with seeing partners who can help explain actions. Because parachutes come in different sizes (15-, 24- and 30-foot diameters), groups of different sizes and abilities can be accommodated easily. The number of participants must be matched with parachute size; this is one activity in which too few participants can be a greater problem than too many.

Individuals with mobility impairments, such as those who use wheelchairs, crutches or braces, can execute movements creatively to emphasize abilities and deemphasize disabilities. When necessary, basic movements with the parachute can be slowed somewhat until all participants successfully develop flow and continuity in each pattern. For beginning instruction and with smaller groups, smaller parachutes and more basic and simpler patterns can be used.

The Parachute

Initially, parachutes were obtained from Air Force or Navy Air surplus stores, parachute riggers and some suppliers of physical education equipment. Because of their popularity as physical education and recreational equipment, most parachutes purchased today are manufactured specifically for use in physical education and recreation programs and activities. In fact, some companies call their parachutes, which come in an appealing range of bright colors, gym canopies. When real parachutes are used, the shrouds are cut off to separate the parachute from the pack.

Circle Ropes

Although elastic circle ropes can be purchased commercially, for safety reasons they are not recommended. Tension developed in the rope creates potentially dangerous situations should the rope slip from a participant's hands.

The easiest and most economical approach is to make a circle rope! Cut a 100-foot length of clothesline in half, and then cut one of the halves in half again, to give a 50-foot rope and two 25-foot ropes. Make each of these into circle ropes by tying the ends with square knots. The resulting circle ropes are extremely strong and can accommodate groups of varying sizes. If a group is too large for the 50-foot rope, untie it and add a 25-foot rope to create one of 75 feet. Small pieces of rope—such as jump ropes—can be tied together to make smaller circles for use by two or three children.

Water Games

Water games provide active, social and fun cool-off activities on hot days and exciting social activities when time hangs long on young hands and minds. In addition, they acclimate the beginning swimmer to the water in pleasant and satisfying ways while challenging good swimmers who have advanced swimming skills. Movement is easier in the water since the body is relatively weightless, and water play may minimize differences in ability between able-bodied and disabled participants.

Water games can be modified easily to suit the needs and abilities of individual participants. For example, experienced swimmers may set up boundary limits that keep them in deep water at all times, and they may or may not be allowed to hang onto the overflow gutters to rest. For nonswimmers or those with limited abilities, games can be confined to water shallow enough for all swimmers to stand with their feet on the bottom and their heads above water.

Accommodations should be made as needed to suit individual abilities; often young participants make excellent suggestions and create variations on their own. The only caveat has to do with water safety: in water more than waist deep, play must be well supervised, lifeguards must be present and rough play must not be allowed.

Many land games may be adapted for water playing, including various footraces and relays and games of

"You've got your whole life ahead, and it runs out pretty fast, so get involved as quickly as possible."[3]

Randy Snow *(Paraplegic)*
Wheelchair Athlete

catch, tag, poison and basketball. Diving for objects or to catch floating objects such as corks is always entertaining. Getting a greased watermelon (use petroleum jelly) out of the water on the opposing team's side of the pool provides strenuous merriment and can involve participants who might have difficulty roughhousing in land games with able-bodied companions. The winning team gets the watermelon!

Games of catch, tag and keep away can easily include swimmers with visual disabilities if rules are modified to require the person who is "it" to make noises or to use noisy objects such as a beep ball. As is true with many other activities presented in this section, only creativity and imagination limit water fun!

Keep Away

When playing Keep Away, players choose sides and play in the shallow end of the pool. The object of this game is for one side to keep the ball away from the other. The game can be adapted for advanced swimmers by playing in the deep end of the pool.

Dodgeball

Dodgeball is particularly enjoyed by youngsters. Choose sides and play in the shallow end of the pool; one group forms a large circle around the second group. Players forming the outside circle attempt to hit players in the inner circle with one or two volleyballs or water polo balls. Players in the middle may walk, run, dodge, duck underwater or swim to avoid being hit. Players who have been hit by the ball move to the outside circle. When all players have been hit, the groups change places, and the procedure is repeated. The last player hit may become captain of the next contest.

To vary the game, time how long it takes each team to eliminate the other. Players who are hit are out—the team that takes the least time to hit all opposing players wins.

Splash

To play Splash, line players up in two rows about 4 feet apart and splash water toward the other line with the palm of the hand. The line that sticks together longest wins. This is a good warm-up (or cool-off) game. Organized splashing games lessen indiscriminate and undesirable splashing at other times.

Handicap Tag

Handicap Tag is a good conditioning game for 5 to 15 players that encourages and promotes water skills. *It* tries to tag other players on the arms or legs as they move about the pool. A player who is tagged continues to move about the pool but cannot use the arm or leg that was tagged. Players who have been tagged several times and cannot move are out of the game. The player staying in the longest wins.

A possible accommodation: Initially handicap all able-bodied players to conform with the disabilities of disabled players.

Stunt Tag

When playing Stunt Tag, a certain part of the body, such as the arm-must be above water to activate the-player; *it* may tag any player who has been activated. Variations include keeping the part out of the water, and having parts both under and out of the water.

Ball Tag

In Ball Tag, *it* tries to tag another player by throwing a ball; the person hit by the ball becomes *it*. Nonswimmers play ball tag in waist-deep water; good swimmers play in deep water.

Neptune Says

Neptune Says players stand in waist- or chest-deep water and face the leader, who calls out skills to be performed. Some commands are prefaced with "Neptune says"; others are called out without "Neptune says." Players are to perform only skills that Neptune says to do. Players moving at the wrong time may be eliminated from the game or acquire points against them so that the player with the lowest number of points wins. Some *Neptune Says* skills include blowing bubbles, jellyfish float, treading water, ducking the head and touching the bottom.

Marco Polo

Although Marco Polo was originally designed for blind and partially sighted players, today it is played almost anyplace people gather to swim. Marco Polo is a simple game of tag, except that it is played in water and players search for each other by sound rather than by sight, a challenging and exciting activity for swimmers of all ages.

Its eyes must be closed at all times. To start the game, *it* usually counts to 10 to give other players time to scatter about the pool. In searching them

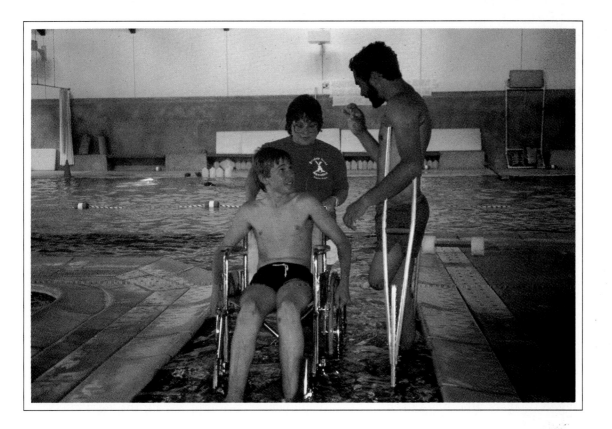

out, *it* calls out *Marco*, and everyone must immediately reply *Polo*. Other rules: No one may hide underwater, and everyone must stay in the designated playing area.

Water Baseball

Water Baseball is played the same way as regular baseball or softball, but the hands are used to bat a plastic whiffle ball, soccer ball, gym ball or Ping-Pong ball. The baseball diamond is set up in all deep water, all shallow water or with only outfielders in deep water.

Sharks and Fishes

When playing Sharks and Fishes, the person designated *it*, the shark, stays in the water. Other players line up outside the pool (or inside the pool along the overflow gutters). At a given signal, all players jump in the water. The shark chases the fishes, and each caught fish is brought to the surface, where it becomes a shark

and pursues other players. The game ends when the last fish is caught.

Accommodations: Fish can begin the game in the water, and the rule about bringing fish to the surface can be changed to accommodate players' abilities and skills.

Portions of this chapter were taken from materials and comments provided by Henning Svendsen and Julian Stein.

REFERENCES

[1] Stein, J. (ed.). *Values of Physical Education, Recreation, and Sports for All* (Reston, VA: American Alliance for Health, Physical Education, Recreation and Dance, Unit on Programs for the Handicapped), p. 20.

[2] Ibid. p. 20.

[3] Maddox, S. (ed.). *Spinal Network: The Total Resource for the Wheelchair Community* (Spinal Network and Sam Maddox, P.O. Box 4162, Boulder, CO, 1987), p. 170.

CHAPTER
9
FITNESS

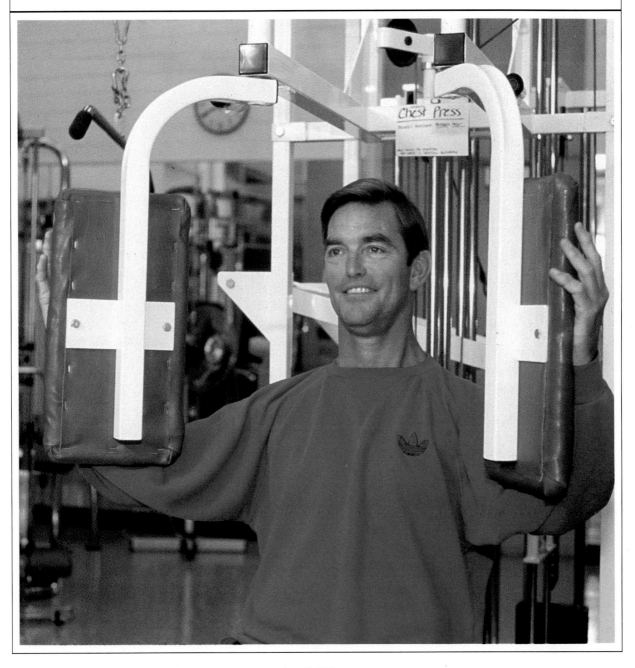

Introduction

Keep fit to stay healthy! As the physical fitness movement sweeps the country, more and more people with disabilities are learning the benefits of keeping fit—the fit person feels better, moves better, has more fun and probably lives longer. In addition, fitness often contributes as much to emotional and psychological well-being as it does to physical health.

Traveling workshops sponsored by the National Handicapped Sports and Recreation Association (NHSRA) have helped increase fitness awareness among people with disabilities. The NHSRA motto explains much of the appeal of fitness activities for people with disabilities—"If I can do this, I can do anything."

A physically fit body functions at an optimal level in emergency situations as well as in everyday living. Athletes do not participate in sport to become fit; rather, athletes become fit in order to participate in sport. Once a person is fit, a sport such as skiing can help maintain some fitness components. However, athletes with disabilities show us just how much fit bodies can do even if a disability is present.

Not everyone wants to become a world-class athlete. For many, health maintenance is a major goal. Everyone needs to exercise to prevent debilitating conditions such as obesity and coronary heart disease, still the nation's number-one killer. As an added incentive, people with physical disabilities need to maintain strength, flexibility and endurance simply to maintain mobility and independence.

What does it take to become fit? Regular exercise. Options range from attaining conventional target heart rates to regular participation in pleasurable, invigorating activities such as gardening and walking. Whatever the choice, the benefits of a fit body are enormous.

"You have to take the responsibility. You are in charge of your life."[1]

Candice Cable-Brooks (Paraplegic)
Wheelchair Athlete

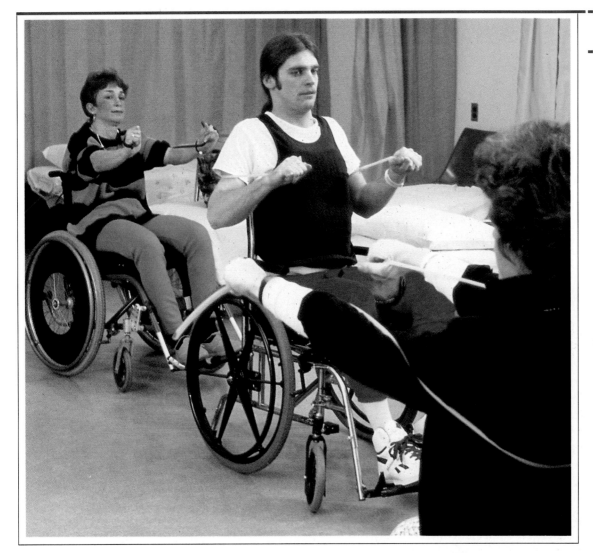

Editors Note:

This text is intended for general reference. The editors, in consultation with physician specialists, strongly recommend that anyone who has a disability consult with a physician before beginning a program of exercise.

Why Keep Fit?

When the body is in good working condition, it feels and works better—we can go farther using less energy while enjoying life more. Regular exercise and a healthful diet mean better mental and physical health—for everyone.

Most people with physical disabilities expend more energy than able-bodied people just in going about their daily activities. In general, when muscle function is lost in any part of the body, the remaining muscles must compensate by working harder and more efficiently. Some persons with mobility impairments must maneuver a bad leg or wheelchair through terrain and over obstacles that are easily covered by able-bodied folks with two good working legs. People with other physical or sensory disabilities experience daily frustrations directly related to their disabilities and often require more energy than most able-bodied people just to get through the rigors of a day's activities.

For these reasons, disabled people often become sedentary and avoid strenuous activity, gradually becoming less fit and less involved in community life. Because until recently few schools or community centers offered programs of vigorous exercise for people with disabilities, many disabled people have never experienced the pleasure of being physically fit.

The loss of fitness resulting from inactivity—and the corresponding loss of social interaction—can itself

> "If you're not in shape, everything is too much work."
>
> George Allen, Chairman
> President's Council on Fitness
> and Sports

become disabling. Inactive disabled persons tend to have less cardiovascular endurance, higher body weight and higher percentages of body fat than either their more active counterparts or disabled athletes.[2]

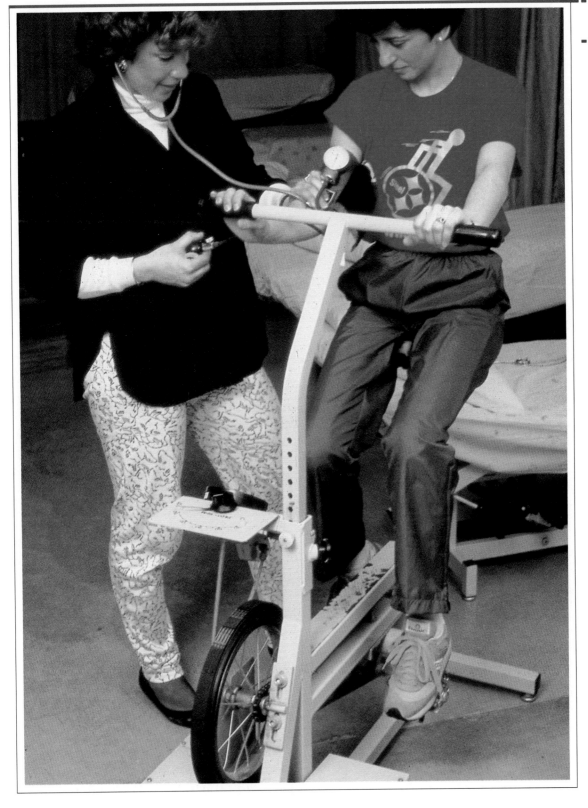

PROFILE

Bill Greene

Bill Greene's reputation lies in his extraordinary commitment and ability as a coach of disabled young people, although he once was a 100-meter wheelchair-racing champion. In fact, he was selected as wheelchair track coach for the 1984 Los Angeles Olympic Games.

In addition to physical fitness, Greene emphasizes the importance of sports in personality development. He has pointed out that handicapped kids are somewhat possessive and self-centered because of all the disability-related attention they get. He teaches his students to give more of themselves, to be less demanding of others, to lose gracefully and that every wish can't be immediately gratified. He pushes kids to do things cooperatively, to work with people, to get things done—skills he believes are sadly lacking among many young disabled people.

Greene knows what it means to be disabled and despondent about personal ability. At 16 he became a paraplegic after he was shot in the spine while trying to break up a fight between two friends. He didn't learn about wheelchair sports until he was 22—until then he had spent a lot of time sitting around, doing nothing and being angry about his disability. According to Greene, "Wheelchair sports would have been terrific motivation for me when I was 16 years old. I could have directed a lot of my hostilities about being disabled into positive channels and got rid of them." In fact, he says that "before participating in wheelchair sports, I had always felt no woman would ever marry me."[3]

Now Greene's wife, Brenda, helps him run New Life Inc., a nationally renowned, after-school sports program in wheelchair basketball, track and field and swimming for disabled young people in the Washington, D.C., area.

But, you may ask, why make the effort to keep fit when it requires more energy and I'm already tired? In general, when the heart, lungs and muscles work harder on a frequent basis, they work longer without tiring and more efficiently, providing reserves for recreation and other leisure activities and making it easier to respond when emergencies occur. The heart becomes stronger and larger, and it requires fewer beats to propel more blood and oxygen toward the muscles. The resting heart rate decreases as the body becomes more fit and uses more oxygen with less effort, thereby conserving energy and delaying muscle fatigue.

The person who is fit tends to be more physically and intellectually alert, better able to concentrate, more emotionally stable and happier than the sedentary person. In addition, research suggests that depressed persons who exercise regularly tend to feel better and use less medication than more sedentary patients.

Furthermore, physical exercise is believed to reduce stress and tension. Participating in a sport or striving to meet a physical fitness goal concentrates the mind wonderfully. A properly stretched and flexed muscle relaxes, and tension flows away. The brain seems to respond similarly.

Beginning an Exercise Program

Usually, the first step in starting an exercise program is to select an activity that exercises large muscle groups. Options include running, swimming, long-distance wheeling, cycling and aerobic dancing. The activity must be right—both doable and enjoyable. *Doable* means affordable and reasonable given one's age, location and physical condition. For example, cycling, a difficult and dangerous activity on congested city streets, may be a good option on bike trails and wide roads in suburbia.

Fitness Assessment Anyone who has been sedentary for a number of years, who has a special condition that could affect an exercise program or who is over 35 years of age should have a physical examination before beginning an exercise program. An assessment of cardiorespiratory fitness should include a stress test, an electrocardiogram and a blood pressure reading.

A fitness assessment is also a good idea, if a health center knowledgeable enough to work with the disability in question is available. In a fitness assessment, muscular strength may be measured through a variety of computerized tests, although many simpler and less sophisticated techniques are available.

> *"Accept total responsibility for what happens to your body . . . you have to become exceedingly well informed."*[4]
>
> Roberta Trieshmann and
> George Hohmann

Safety Exercise in high heat and humidity can be hazardous for anyone, but it can be especially so for some disabled persons. According to Kathy Fensterman-Normansell, a NHSRA consultant, heat will quickly fatigue a person with multiple sclerosis or muscular dystrophy, shortening the workout period. Because of disturbances in sweating mechanisms, persons with high-level spinal cord injuries may have difficulty cooling their bodies and must be very careful in hot and humid conditions. As a general rule when exercising, but especially during hot weather, people should drink plenty of water prior to and during exercise, wear protective clothing and spray cool water on the back of the neck, head and face. A headband soaked in cold water helps dissipate body heat during exercise.[5] Exercising in very cool weather or water also can be harmful, because cold muscles are less flexible and more prone to injury. In addition, very cool temperatures may increase muscle spasticity in persons with cerebral palsy. People with spinal cord injuries are susceptible to hypothermia and must take precautions when exercising, especially in cold and rainy weather.

Five Steps to Fitness A solid exercise program usually involves five steps: warm-up, stretching, full exercise, cool down and final stretching. These steps are no different from training regimens used by able-bodied people.

Warm-up prepares the muscles, heart and lungs for an increased workload in which the heart gradu-

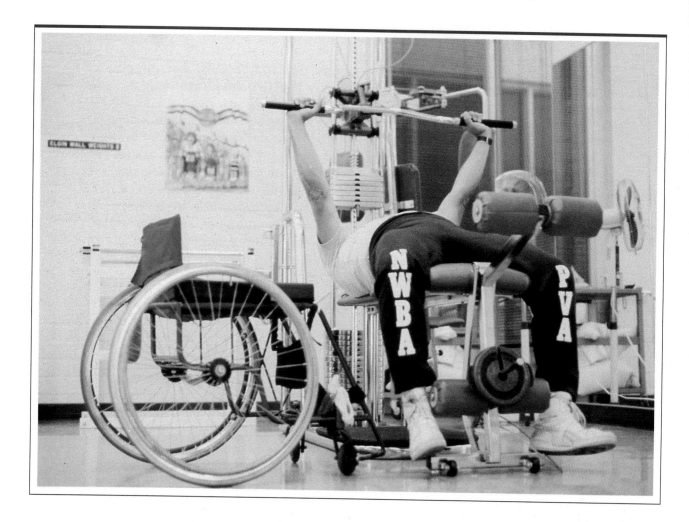

ally begins beating harder and faster, the lungs send out more oxygen, body temperature increases and muscles gradually increase their rate of contraction and relaxation.

Warm-up makes *stretching* easier because muscles are warm and less easily injured. Stretching brings the muscle into its longest position. A lot of muscle contracting, which shortens the muscles, takes place during a workout. The stretching before and after the workout helps to balance out the muscle shortening caused by the contractions and reduces the likelihood of injury and muscle soreness. Since different disabilities and different sports affect how muscles work, stretching exercises should be responsive to individual needs.

Full exercise involves somewhat hard exertion of major muscle groups for at least 20 minutes in which the heartbeat is maintained at 60 to 80 percent of maximum rate. After full exercise, the *cool-down* process eases the workload, reversing the workout process without unduly stressing the heart and other muscles by a sudden stop.

Final stretching, although often neglected, is an important part of the process. During intense exercise, lactic acid may accumulate in the muscles, causing cramping or aching after exercise. Stretching immediately after exercise helps move lactic acid out of the muscles; if muscles begin to ache several hours later, more stretching may help, but not more exercising!

Fitness Facilities

Fitness facilities, which can be found in YMCAs, schools and universities, community recreation centers and private health clubs, can be an excellent source of fitness instruction and equipment. For persons with mobility impairments, the first issue is getting into and around the facility—do curbs have cuts in place and are showers, restrooms and equipment accessible? Staff should be asked whether they are comfortable working with people with disabilities and about their experience training persons with the disability in question. The financial stability of private clubs and the cleanliness and quality of facilities and equipment also should be examined.

PROFILE

Kirk Bauer

Kirk Bauer, the executive director of the National Handicapped Sports and Recreation Association, is dedicated to improving the health and physical fitness of disabled people. Skiing is Bauer's sport; in fact, he is a certified professional ski instructor. A single-leg amputee due to a war wound, Bauer is one of the few disabled persons nationwide who has earned professional ski instructor certification.

Bauer's professional dedication to health and physical fitness for disabled people has resulted in a long list of accomplishments and awards—the President's Fitness Award, presented by the President's Council on Physical Fitness and Sports; an award from the American Academy of Physician Assistants for outstanding service in rehabilitating American veterans; and the 1986 Healthy American Fitness Leader Award, from the President's Council on Physical Fitness and Sports, for extraordinary commitment to health and physical fitness in society. Bauer has also been appointed by the President to serve on the President's Committee on Employment of People with Disabilities.

Bauer firmly believes in the importance of sport for people with disabilities: "During my 17 years with NHSRA, I have come to know the dedication and hard work of many people who truly believe they can make a difference. Many are meeting and overcoming their own challenges head on while working to help others do the same. NHSRA's motto, 'If I can do this, I can do anything,' becomes an actuality for most people who do actively participate in sports and recreation."

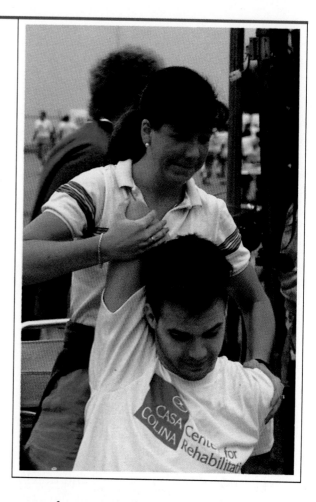

Flexibility

Maintaining a full range of motion helps disabled people maintain mobility and independence. Fensterman-Normansell points out that a person with a flexible body has a lower risk of injury and performs daily living routines more easily. Flexibility also helps prevent the disabling contractures of cerebral palsy, in which the limbs tightly contract in an inward position.[6]

To avoid injury, any person with spastic paralysis or loss of sensation should stretch slowly and carefully. As a matter of fact, everyone should stretch slowly and carefully. Only static stretches (held for a period of time) are recommended; moving stretches are likely to produce soreness and injury. Those who spend most of their time sitting should regularly stretch each hip in a direction opposite to the sitting position. Persons with leg amputations may need to modify their positions somewhat to stretch the remaining muscles of the amputated leg. Again, NHSRA manuals and videotapes outline precautions and highlight stretches of special importance to people with disabilities.

Aerobic Dance

Dance is a popular fitness routine. Because it is set to music and it's fun and easy to learn, people leave feeling great. Exercise to music through jazzercise, dancercise or aerobic workouts is becoming popular for men and women of all age groups, including those with disabilities. The benefits of such workouts include improved range of motion and flexibility, strength, endurance and a more efficient heart and lungs. Additional benefits may include better posture, help in weight control and increased feelings of well-being.

With minor modifications, most persons with physical and sensory disabilities can participate in regular aerobic dance programs. In general, Kathy Fensterman-Normansell recommends that wheelchair users substitute rapid, rhythmical arm movements for leg movements. As much muscle mass as possible should be used to increase the aerobic effort.[7]

Persons with weakened or reduced functioning in muscle groups frequently change the muscle group being worked to avoid cutting the workout short because of premature fatigue. Persons with poor coordination (such as some persons who have cerebral palsy), on the other hand, need to repeat the same movement for prolonged periods and at a slower rate to avoid awkward transitions between movements that could hamper the aerobic effort. A chair should also be available to use in case of loss of balance or fatigue.

Often persons with hearing impairments learn most easily by watching; those with visual impairments usually need detailed, clear and precise verbal instructions. Sometimes instructions are understood best when the instructor physically moves the dancer into desired positions.

In general, the beginning dancer should not concentrate on style. Rather, keep moving and stretching all major body parts. Style comes later with practice!

NHSRA has developed a set of manuals and videotapes that provide disabled persons and aerobic instructors with information on aerobic dance adaptations and precautions. The 30-minute videotapes are specifically designed to help people with disabilities obtain maximum success and benefit from aerobic dance workouts.

Muscular Strength and Endurance Training

In addition to aerobic exercise, muscular endurance and strength development are important components of a total fitness program. Muscular strength is primarily increased through a well-rounded weight-training program that may involve exercises such as sit-ups and pull-ups. Endurance is developed through many repetitions of weight-lifting exercises using low resistance and through logging many miles each week in activities such as swimming, cycling, wheeling or running.

While weight training cannot reverse a progressive neuromuscular disability, good muscular strength makes daily living activities and recreational pursuits easier and more enjoyable. In addition, it is now generally accepted that under proper supervision, gymnasts, swimmers, basketball players and others significantly improve their athletic performances through weight training for strength development.

Fensterman-Normansell recommends that wheelchair users pay special attention to strengthening upper-back and abdominal muscles to maintain erect posture. Likewise, leg amputees should strengthen lower-back and abdominal muscles to maintain good pelvic and lower-back alignment. She reports that, contrary to popular wisdom, there is no evidence that extensive strength training leads to increased muscle spasticity in persons with cerebral palsy, although stretching routines always should be incorporated into their workouts. It is also important to balance exercise of muscle groups. As an example, if the exercise is to bend the arm, then the opposing exercise to extend the arm must be performed.[8]

Techniques to develop strength and endurance vary with the ability and preference of each participant. In general, free weights are not recommended for use by persons with weak or reduced muscle control or coordination difficulties. Spotters must always be present when an individual works with free weights as they can be easily dropped, causing injury. In addition, free weights can be difficult to manipulate correctly.

Hand and ankle weights, wall pulley systems or self-contained exercise machines are preferable and safer approaches to strength and endurance development. Rubber tubing of varying diameters and resistance (try bicycle inner tubes) are a low-cost and portable means of strength and endurance training. Examples of tubing use are provided in NHSRA videotapes and instructional manuals.

Weight-training activities can be accomplished by transferring from a wheelchair to multi-station, single-unit weight machines; usually no special equipment is necessary. Individuals who cannot transfer from wheelchairs can perform modified lifts and other activities directly from their chairs. Training can take place at any club that has accessible facilities and an instructor to provide advice.

Principles of Training

Athletes preparing for competition must keep their overall goals firmly in mind. If the goal is to run a long-distance endurance race, then training must be directed toward that endurance goal. If the athlete is a thrower of discus, shot or javelin, then the athlete must follow training programs designed to improve performances in that event. Training today is highly specific. By following basic principles of training, athletes increase their chances of success.

The *Principle of Specificity of Training* states that athletic training must be highly specific to the sport and to particular requirements and strategies of that sport. To become a better runner or swimmer, the athlete must run or swim. Motor learning and fitness obtained in one activity will not necessarily transfer to another.

The *Principle of Overload/Stress* requires that cardiovascular and muscular-skeletal systems be stressed in each training session if highest performance is to be achieved over time. Depending on the goal of training, this may mean reaching and maintaining an accelerated heartbeat or lifting weights that overload the muscle.

The *Principle of Progression* means that resistance is increased as muscles gain strength. Activities must be gradually increased to greater intensity, higher frequency and over longer periods of time to maintain the training load needed to improve training effects. The athlete must set daily, weekly, monthly and even yearly goals to be successful in the event of choice.

The *Principle of Recovery and Rest* indicates that athletes cannot work every day at an intense level. Muscles need rest, and the fuel supply for the muscle must be replenished, a process that requires 24 to 48 hours. Severe training days must be

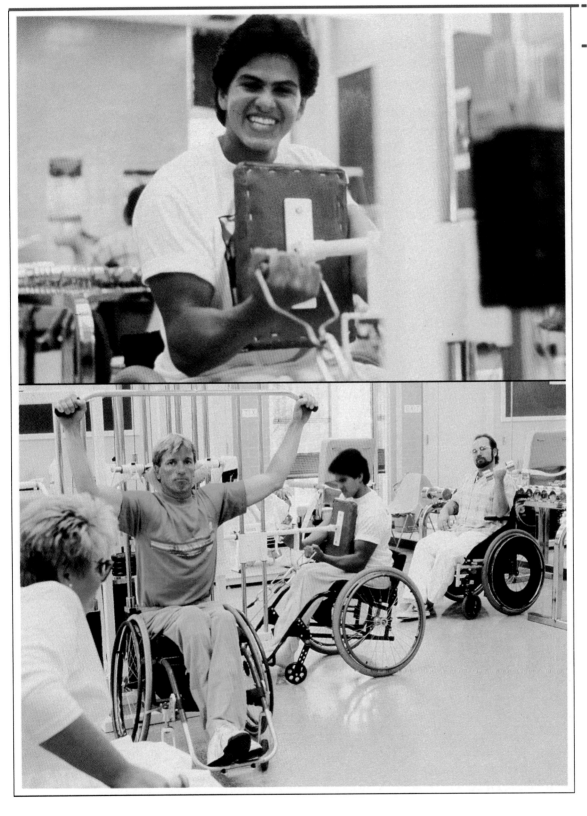

followed by rest, very light training or emphasis on other physical components or different muscles and muscle groups.

The *Principle of Diminishing Returns* means that as an athlete's performance improves, the rate of improvement drops. As athletes continue to train beyond a period of weeks and months, and perhaps even years, they approach their maximal potential, and their rate of improvement gradually levels off.

Patty Miller and Julian Stein provided comments on this chapter.

REFERENCES

[1] Maddox, S. (ed.). *Spinal Network: The Total Resource for the Wheelchair Community* (Spinal Network and Sam Maddox, P.O. Box 4162, Boulder, CO), p. 147.

[2] Fensterman-Normansell, K. "A Brief Overview of the Need for Fitness and Simple Modifications for Disabled People." Paper prepared for the National Handicapped Sports and Recreation Association (1986), Washington, D.C., p. 1.

[3] Allen, A. *Sports for the Handicapped* (New York: Walker and Company, 1981), p. 29.

[4] Maddox, op. cit. p. 75.

[5] Fensterman-Normansell, K. "Integrated Aerobics, Joint Programming for Disabled and Able-Bodied," *Aerobics and Fitness*, 4:6 (1986), p. 24.

[6] Fensterman-Normansell, op. cit. p. 23.

[7] Ibid. p. 6.

[8] Ibid. p. 7.

Appendix

National Organizations and Resources

American Athletic Association
of the Deaf (AAAD)
　　Richard Caswell
　　3916 Lantern Drive
　　Silver Spring, MD 20902

American Alliance for Health,
Physical Education, Recreation
and Dance (AAHPERD)
　　1900 Association Drive
　　Reston, VA 22091

American Blind Bowling
Association, Inc.
　　150 N. Bellaire Avenue
　　Louisville, KY 40206

American Wheelchair Bowling
Association
　　Daryl Pilster
　　N54 W. 15858 Larkspur Lane
　　Menomonee Falls, WI 53051

American Wheelchair Table
Tennis Association
　　Edward Morrison, President
　　166 Haas Avenue
　　Paramus, NJ 07652

Archery Sports Section
　　Sister Kenny Institute
　　Susan Hagel
　　800 East 28th at Chicago Ave.
　　Minneapolis, MN 55407

Canadian Wheelchair Sports
Association
　　333 River Road
　　Ottawa, Ontario,
　　Canada K1L 8H9

Council for Disabled Sailors,
American Sailing Association
Foundation
　　60 Padanaram Road, Unit 16
　　Danbury, CT 06810

Courage Center, Department of
Sports, Physical Education and
Recreation
　　3915 Golden Valley Road
　　Golden Valley, MN 55422

Challenge Golf
　　Peter Longo
　　P.O. Box 27283
　　Tempe, AZ 85282

Eastern Amputee Athletic
Association
　　Jack Graff, President
　　2080 Ennabrock Road
　　North Bellmore, NY 11710

Handicapped Scuba Association
　　Jim Gatacre
　　1104 El Prado
　　San Clemente, CA 92672

International Bicycle Tours
　　12 Mid Place
　　Chappaqua, NY 10514

International Foundation for
Wheelchair Tennis
　　Peter Burwash
　　2203 Timerlouch Place, Suite
　　126
　　The Woodlands, TX 77380

International Wheelchair Road
Racers Club, Inc.
　　Joseph W. Dowling, President
　　30 Myano Lane
　　Stamford, CT 06902

International Sports
Organization for the Disabled
(ISOD)
　　Stoke Mandeville Sports
　　Stadium
　　Harvey Road,
　　Aylesbury, Bucks, England
　　HP2 1PP

Mission Bay Aquatic Center
　　1001 Santa Clara Point
　　San Diego, CA 92109

National Beep Baseball
Association
　　512 8th Avenue, N.E.
　　Minneapolis, MN 55413
　　or--9623 Spencer Highway
　　La Porte, TX 77571

National Foundation of
Wheelchair Tennis
　　Brad Parks, Director
　　940 Calle Amanecer, Suite B
　　San Clemente, CA 92672

National Handicapped Sports
and Recreation Association
(NHSRA)
　　Ron Hernley, President
　　Farragut Station
　　P.O. Box 33141
　　Washington, D.C. 20033

National Ocean Access Project
　　410 Severn Avenue, Suite 306
　　Annapolis, MD 21403

National Outward Bound Office
　　384 Field Point Road
　　Greenwich, CT 06830

National Wheelchair Athletic
Association (NWAA)
　　1604 E. Pike Ave.
　　Colorado Springs, CO 80909

National Wheelchair Basketball
Association (NWBA)
　　Stan Labanowich,
　　Commissioner
　　110 Seaton Building
　　University of Kentucky
　　Lexington, KY 40506

National Wheelchair Shooting
Federation(NWAA)
　　545 Ridge Road
　　Wilbraham, MA 01095

National Wheelchair Softball
Association
　　Jon Speake, Commissioner
　　P.O. Box 22478
　　Minneapolis, MN 55422

North American Riding for the
Handicapped Association
    P.O. Box 33150
    Denver, CO 80223

Physically Challenged
Swimmers of America/NWAA
    Joan Karpuk
    22 William Street #225
    South Glastonbury, CT 06073

*United States Amputee
Athletic Association
(USAAAA)
    Richard Bryant
    149-A Belle Forest Circle
    Nashville, TN 37221

*United States Association for
Blind Athletes (USABA)
    Art Copeland
    55 West California Avenue
    Beach Haven Park, NJ 08008

*United States Cerebral Palsy
Athletic Association
    34518 Warren Road, Suite 264
    Westland, MI 48185

United States Organization for
Disabled Athletes
    161 Westfield Circle
    Danville, CA 94562

United States Quad Rugby
Association
    Brad Mickelson
    2418 Fall Creek Court
    Grand Forks, ND 58201

U.S. Wheelchair Racquet
Sports Association
    Chip Parmelly
    1941 Viento Verano Drive
    Diamond Bar, CA 91765

United States Rowing
Association
    251 N. Illinois Street,
    Suite 980
    Indianapolis, IN 46204

United States Wheelchair
Weight Lifting
Federation/NWAA
    Bill Hens
    39 Michael Place
    Levittown, PA 19057

Vinland National Center
    P.O. Box 308
    Loretto, MN 55357

Wheelchair Athletics of America
    Judy Einbinder
    8114 Buffalo Speedway
    Houston, TX 77025

Wilderness Inquiry
    1313 SE Fifth Street,
    Box 84
    Minneapolis, MN 55414

Winter Park Handicap Sports
and Competition Program
    Box 36, Winter Park, CO
    80482

Other:

WEIGHT TRAINING
Casa Colina/Work It Out
Program,
    255 Bonita Ave.,
    Pomona, CA 91767

FOOTBALL
City of Santa Barbara
Recreation Department,
    P.O. Drawer P-P
    Santa Barbara, CA 93102

KAYAKING
Nantahala Outdoor Center,
    Star Route, Box 68,
    Bryson City, NC 28713

National Institute of Health
Fitness Center,
    9000 Wisconsin Ave.,
    Bldg. T-39,
    Bethesda, MD 20205

Acknowledgements

Many individuals and organizations have been extremely helpful in contributing materials, offering suggestions, reviewing text and making photographs available for use in this book. We are particularly indebted to Nancy Crase, Managing Editor, *Sports 'n Spokes'* magazine (a publication of the Paralyzed Veterans of America) for her invaluable assistance in text review and for allowing us to access *Sports 'n Spokes'* extensive photographic library. We also wish to acknowledge the extraordinary contributions of Julian U. Stein and Elizabeth Defay for their assistance in all aspects of the development of this book.

Others most deserving of special appreciation are: Steve McCarty, *Impressive Images*; Greg Lais, *Wilderness Inquiry*; Jim Salmon, *Odyssey Productions*; Stewart Halperin, *Stewart Halperin Studios*; Jerry Johnston, *Canadian Handicapped Sports Association*; Olga Byll, *the Hospital for Sick Children*; Marti Cushing, *Vinland National Center*; Roxanne Fischetti, *Veterans Administration*; Robert Szyman, *Courage Center*; Nikki Gramatikos, *Casa Colina, Inc.*; Bill Barry, *Amputee Soccer International*; Kathy Corbin, *Never Say Never*; Pauline Egan, *Harmorville Rehabilitation Center*; Gary Baker, *Parkersburg, West Virginia*; Gay Clement and Roger Neppel, *United States Association for Blind Athletes*; Tana Cunningham, *National Ocean Access Project*; George Depontis, *CAT CAM*; Suzanne Green, *Disabled Rowing*; Bill Hamilton, *Santa Barbara Recreation Department*; Brad Hedrick, *University of Illinois Rehabilitation Education Center*; Diane Hottendorf and Sue Gill, *Gallaudet University*; Chris Keim, *Special Olympics Rowing*; John Klein, *PGA professional golfer, La Mesa, California*; James Mastro, *Fridley, Minnesota*; Dean Mellway, *Canadian Wheelchair Sports Association*; Brad Mikkelsen, *United States Quad Rugby Association*; Michael Mushett, *United States Cerebral Palsy Athletic Association*; Dana Nadeau, *the Sharf Marketing Group*; Wendy Parks, *National Foundation of Wheelchair Tennis*; Nina Perry, *National Handicapped Sports and Recreation Association*; E. Louise Priest, *Council for National Cooperation in Aquatics*; Jane Stanfield, *North American Riding for the Handicapped*; Susan Sygall, *Mobility International USA*; Bob Wilson, *National Amputee Golf Association*; Bob Douglas, *Therapeutic Riding Center*; Janet Pomeroy, *Recreation Center for the Handicapped*; and Martin Naucler, *Rep. Sigma HB*.

Finally, we wish to thank William Hillman, Jr., Washington, D.C.; Kay Ellis, *U.S. National Park Service*; Stan Labanowich, *National Wheelchair Basketball Association*; Peter Longo, *professional golfer*; Patty Miller, *NHSRA*; Grace Reynolds, *YMCA*; Wendy Shugol, Lee Lawrence and our Swedish colleagues Gert Engström and Sven-Olof Brattgård for their assistance.

The Editors

We also wish to express our appreciation to:

Image Typesetting, Orlando, Florida • *Page composition.*
Magna Graphic, Lexington, Kentucky • *Color separations.*
Mid-City Lithographers, Lake Forest, Illinois • *Cover printing.*
W. A. Kruger Co., New Berlin, Wisconsis • *Printing and binding.*

Photographic Contributors

Amputee Soccer International, pp. 28 (T), 28 (B), 29
*Frederick Anderson, p. 59
Canadian Handicapped Sports Association, pp. 178 (TL), 178 (TR), 178 (B), 179
Canadian Wheelchair Sports Association, pp. 12, 65 (T), 67 (B)
CAT CAM, p. 10
Council for National Cooperation in Aquatics, pp. 126 (B), 128, 129, 131
Courage Center, pp. 8, 23, 36 (B), 191, 198
Gallaudet University
    *Seny Norasingh, p. 186
Harmorville Rehabilitation Center, pp. 57 (T), 111, 219, 221
Hospital for Sick Children
    *Rhoda Baer, pp. 200, 201, 205
    *David Hathcox, pp. 199, 203
Impressive Images
    *Steve McCarty (Photographer), pp. 2, 13, 14, 21 (T), 61, 138, 145, 149, 208 (T), 208 (B), 213, 214
Inspire '85, p. 136
*John Klein, p. 48 (T, B)
*James Mastro, pp. 4, 5, 7
Mobility International–USA, pp. 105, 215
Mission Bay, Backcover (R)
National Amputee Golf Association, p. 46
National Foundation of Wheelchair Tennis, pp. 109, 127, 212
National Handicapped Sports and Recreation Association
*Brooks Dodge, pp. 169, 171, front cover (B,L)
National Ocean Access Project, pp. 107, 122
Never Say Never
    *Sandy Miller (Photographer), p. 47
North American Riding for the Handicapped, p. 98 (T, B)
Odyssey Productions
    *Jim Salmon (Photographer), pp. 181, 182, 184, 189, Back cover (middle)
Santa Barbara Recreation Department
*Alan Degasis, pp. 17, 18, 19
Special Olympics Rowing, pp. 118, 119
Sports 'n Spokes
    *Nancy Crase and Curt Beamer (Photographers), pp. 9, 33, 39, 55, 63, 64,65 (B), 68, 100, 116 (T), 120 (T), 126 (T), 135, 137 (B), 142, 147, 151 (T), 151 (B), 153 (B), 155 (B), 156 (T), 156 (B), 157 (TR), 157 (TL), 157 (B), 158, 159 (T), 160 (TR), 161 (TL), 161 (TR), 162 (T), 163, 174, front cover (R), backcover (B,L)
*Julian Stein, pp. 210, 211
Stewart Halperin Studios
    *Stewart Halperin (Photographer), pp. 21 (B), 25 (B), 51 (BL), 67 (T), 70 (B), 71, 116 (B), 190, 209
Sharf Marketing Group
    *Herbert Schriebel (Photographer) (courtesy of ChapStick™ lip balm), p. 167
Swedish Photographers
    *Martin Naucler (Photographer), pp. 15, 36 (T), 38, 97, 101, 113, 120 (B), 124, 137 (TL), 139, 148, 155 (T), 160 (TL), 195
    *Claës Lewenhaupt (Photographer), p. viii
United States Association for Blind Athletes, pp. 51 (BR), 69, 115, 132, 141, 146 (B), 176 (T)
United States Cerebral Palsy Athletic Association, pp. 24, 25 (T)
United States Quad Rugby Association, pp. 27, 31
University of Illinois, pp. 22, 143 (B), 143 (R), 153 (T), back cover (T,L)
Veterans Administration, pp. 37, 42, 57 (B), 159 (B), 162 (B), 165, 168, 170, 173, 174 (TL), 174 (TR)
Vinland National Center, pp. 93, 94, 95, 193, front cover (T,L)
White House Photographer, pp. x, 101
Wilderness Inquiry, pp. 73, 75 (T), 75 (B), 77, 78, 79 (T), 79 (B), 80, 83 (TL), 83 (TR), 83 (B), 85, 87 (T), 87 (BL), 89 (T), 89 (B), 90 (L), 90 (R), 91, 103, 104, 176 (B), front cover (middle)

A 9
B 0
C 1
D 2
E 3
F 4
G 5
H 6
I 7
J 8